Grantwriting, Fundraising, and Partnerships

Grantwriting, Fundraising, and Partnerships

Strategies That Work!

Karen B. Ruskin
Charles M. Achilles

CORWIN PRESS, INC.
A Sage Publications Company
Thousand Oaks, California

For information address:

Corwin Press, Inc.
A Sage Publications Company
2455 Teller Road
Thousand Oaks, California 91320

SAGE Publications Ltd.
6 Bonhill Street
London EC2A 4PU
United Kingdom

SAGE Publications India Pvt. Ltd.
M-32 Market
Greater Kailash I
New Delhi 110 048 India

Printed in the United States of America

Library of Congress Cataloging-in-Publication Data

Ruskin, Karen B.
    Grantwriting, fundraising, and partnerships : strategies that work
/ Karen B. Ruskin, Charles M. Achilles.
        p.   cm.
    Includes bibliographical references and index.
    ISBN 0-8039-6220-7 — ISBN 0-8039-6221-5 (pbk.)
    1. Educational fund raising—United States. 2. Proposal writing
for grants—United States. 3. Proposal writing in education—United
States.   I. Achilles, Charles M.   II. Title.
LC243.A1R87   1995
379.1'3—dc20   95-33093

This book is printed on acid-free paper.

95 96 97 98 99 10 9 8 7 6 5 4 3 2 1

Corwin Press Production Editor: S. Marlene Head

Contents

Preface

This book is written for teachers and administrators who are developing new sources of funding for school and districtwide projects. Funding and proposal development information presented will help other stakeholders who work daily with schools to achieve success in the grantwriting process. Funding obtained through the recommended grantwriting and comprehensive fundraising strategies will provide the seed monies to implement new and vital materials and services for students in the classroom.

This book is *not* specifically about federal grant programs; however, *general* ideas and tips included here will help the grantseeker at all levels.

We hope that teachers and administrators, together with organizations within their communities, will make those much-needed changes in schools. (To that end, this book is dedicated.) In the group of essential stakeholders in the revitalization of America's schools are parents, students, administrators, school board members, businesspeople, and foundations. Educators must assume the leadership role in important school change projects by developing working partnerships to obtain the resources that we will use to make those changes. Grant information presented in this handbook will be a useful tool for this challenging endeavor.

The focus of this handbook is the conceptualization, writing, and marketing of grant proposals, specifically for educators. The reader will have the opportunity to compare examples of funded and non-funded grant proposals, which will provide helpful models for proposal development. Funded proposals should be used as reader guides because they provide insights about those proposals that have been selected for funding by grant administrators and about the selection process itself. Proposal-writing tips, recommendations about how to develop a budget for the proposal, and strategies for marketing your ideas are provided.

In the Resources at the end of the handbook, we offer information about a wide range of education grants to fund classroom, schoolwide, and collaborative projects. Some foundations that fund large-scale education projects are identified in Resource D. Bibliographic materials provide additional assistance in identifying potential funders.

Acknowledgments

Thanks to so many individuals and organizations for their contributions to this ambitious undertaking. Special thanks to Kathryn Carey, Grants Manager of the American Honda Foundation, who so generously provided her insights into the grant selection process for inclusion in this book; to Dr. Del Roy of the Hitachi Foundation, who contributed an excellent critique of both accepted and rejected proposals; to Bob Fitzpatrick, Vice President and Treasurer of the Procter & Gamble Fund, for his in-depth responses to a lengthy interview; and to Mrs. Ann Manley, Executive Director of the Dr. Phillips Foundation, for her perspectives on grant organization.

A special note of thanks goes to Dr. María Shelton, Director of the National Ed.D. Program for Educational Leaders at Nova Southeastern University, for her encouragement. Thanks also to Nova colleagues Dr. Ron Newell, Dr. John Long, and Dr. Gloria Kuchinskas, who have supported this endeavor.

Pam Masters, Director of the Enterprise Ambassador Program, which is a successful partnership with Wendy's founder Dave Thomas, provided guidelines for collaborative ventures. Judy Meyer, Director of the Office of Business and Citizen Partnerships, Florida Department of Education, gave generously of her time to discuss this project, as did Vicki Gillespie of Bank South to discuss the Atlanta Partnership for Goals 2000.

Thanks to Dr. Jim Kraft and Dr. Fern Aefsky, who contributed articles about the funding process while they were both school administrators and doctoral candidates at Nova Southeastern University.

Mary Joan Connors, a successful proposal writer who is a language arts teacher in the Dade County, Florida schools, provided helpful lists of grants that she has used to fund a myriad of classroom and districtwide projects.

Dean Richard Goldman of the Center for the Advancement of Education at Nova Southeastern University, Fort Lauderdale, Florida, provided kind support. Nova professors Dr. David Flight and Dr. Joan Mignerey, colleagues and mentors, provided helpful feedback.

I also acknowledge the assistance and encouragement of teachers and administrators, my students at Nova Southeastern University. From them, I have gained important insights into the needs of teachers and administrators for information about the grantwriting process. For this handbook, topics were either selected or eliminated as a response to feedback from students and in response to expressed concerns of the many educators with whom I have discussed the need for additional dollars to make changes in their schools.

On a personal note, this book could not have been written without the invaluable assistance of my son, Mike Somlo, who provided an indispensable ingredient—the computer notebook used to write this handbook. Thanks to my brother, Bill, and sister, Adrienne Kamin, for their patient support, and to Dr. George Stevens for his enduring friendship.

Finally, thanks go to Nancy Chamberlain of DeKalb, Illinois, who helped "shape up" the final product, and to Joanna Warder of Geneva, New York, and Ray Kessler of Computer Associates, Pompano Beach, Florida, whose technical assistance enabled me to complete the book.

KAREN B. RUSKIN
FORT LAUDERDALE, FLORIDA

In addition to the above acknowledgments, I wish to thank Dr. Ernest Brewer and Dr. Joy Fuhriman, my coauthors of *Finding Funding* (Corwin Press), for their ideas that I may have incorporated into this text.

CHARLES M. ACHILLES
GENEVA, NEW YORK

About the Authors

Karen B. Ruskin, Ed.D., has taught courses in grantsmanship and conducted seminars for educators on resource identification and proposal writing with a focus on private funding sources. She currently advises school administrators in the design, implementation, and evaluation of successful school improvement projects, and she consults on obtaining nonbudgeted dollars for project funding.

Dr. Ruskin has drawn on her experiences as teacher, grants recipient, school administrator, grants lecturer, grantwriter, and grant researcher to provide comprehensive information about the grant-award process. For more information, Dr. Ruskin may be contacted at 4821 Coconut Creek Parkway, Suite 132, Coconut Creek, Florida 33063, (954) 968-6220.

Charles M. Achilles, Ed.D., has been active in writing projects and securing sources of funding cooperatively with school and agency leaders. He is coauthor of *Finding Funding* (Corwin Press), a book that emphasizes the development of project ideas for federal funding sources. He frequently teaches proposal development courses, seminars, and workshops. He has secured personal grant support for his research and development work continuously since 1968, and he has authored, coauthored, or contributed to projects totaling more than $100 million.

1

Planning a Proposal: The Beginning

To give away money . . . is an easy matter and in any man's power. But to decide to whom to give it and how much and when, and for what purpose and how, is neither in every man's power nor an easy matter.

ARISTOTLE

Chapter Highlights

- Asking the Right Questions
- What Makes a Successful Grantseeker
- Positive Steps to a Successful Proposal
- Identifying Funders
- Writing the Letter of Intent
- Writing a Cover Letter

This book is about how you may magnify the impact of your school's activities by expanding the sources of support for school-related efforts. One obvious way to do this is to write a successful proposal for a grant. That is the main focus of this book.

There are other ways to expand your impact. You can establish partnerships with area businesses and agencies. You might work closely with persons in other education organizations, such as people from other schools or from higher education, to extend the impact of each party. The current trend toward site-level decisions requires teachers and principals to know more and more about generating resources to extend school services. This will occasionally work with local community groups and agencies, even with individuals (e.g., volunteers) who may provide in-kind contributions (i.e., not hard cash, but support and "sweat equity" that has a dollar value). Your school site may become a center for student teaching or for interns in teaching, administration, counseling, social services, and so on.

When politicians and policymakers develop new programs or redirect resources of current programs, there is a concurrent opportunity to seek funds for that program. These funds may be available through federal, regional, state, area, or local sources; the sources may be private (e.g., foundations) or public (e.g., government). Teachers may cooperate with higher education faculty to conduct research or to evaluate programs. Each of these efforts is an *increase* in the resource pool of the local site, but the ultimate way to extend your agency's impact is to seek and get external funding support.

Proposal writing is a craft, a science, and an art. As a craftsman or craftswoman, your capability in applying knowledge about the process of obtaining funding will improve through trial and error. As a scientist, you will study rigorously both the sources for funding support and the problems that you wish to solve. The proposal development process can also serve strategic and tactical planning activities and an evaluation function for your agency. As the artist, your art form, the actual proposal document, is the matching of *your* ideas with the interests of the funding source. Proposal writing is also an art because the author brings his or her own life interpretations to the creative process. Your own experience and your imagination combine to dictate how you will approach the myriad challenges of proposal writing and which options you will select from a broad range of possibilities.

As you learn more about foundations, and as you broaden your ideas to expand the number of students, teachers, and entire school enterprises that will benefit from your grant, you will also provide innovative opportunities for funding. New ways of thinking, new methods of proceeding, new outlooks, and new challenges may well be outgrowths of a reconceptualization of the project that you are proposing. Creative and technical ends of proposal writing are discussed in this handbook.

In chapter 1, we raise some issues and offer some brief introductory comments that we expand upon in later chapters. In the later chapters, we provide examples and details that will lead the grant seeker to correct sources of support and to the development of a successful proposal to obtain the support.

Asking the Right Questions

Proposal writing requires reflection and questioning. Good questions help you to organize and develop your ideas and then allow you to "check off" at the end to see if you've forgotten anything. There are three times to take stock by answering questions: (a) before you start, (b) while you are developing the proposal, and (c) just before you send the document for final production.

Questions That Provide Structure for Your Grant

Some of the following questions will help you in providing structure for your grant proposal:

1. What problem needs attention *and* added fund support for its resolution?
2. What do others think about this idea?
3. What do you need to do to be eligible for this grant?
4. Is the grant open to personnel at your grade level or type of school (public or private)?
5. Does the problem you plan to resolve through funding match the priorities of the funder?
6. Can you carry out your project in your school alone, or would it be improved if it is a collaborative venture?
7. Is the grant an outright award or a matching grant?
8. Do you have adequate information about current budgets that are (or may become) available to assist you in achieving your goals?
9. What data do you have about this problem?
10. Does this grant activity require the principal's or school board's approval? (All projects should employ collaborative effort and communications about the work.)

Once you have answered these questions, you are ready to begin your search for a funding source for your idea. The bibliography provided in this handbook provides some resources to get you started. Other funding sources also should be consulted for information as you develop a list of possibilities for support. You will want to tailor each proposal to meet the particular requirements of the funder.

Mary Joan Connors, a language arts teacher in the Dade County (Florida) Public Schools, has written numerous successful proposals. She suggests that you ask and answer the following questions before writing a proposal:

1. What kind of grant are you seeking?
2. Does it require school board approval?
3. Have you discussed it with a colleague or someone from the Office of Grants Administration?
4. Must you be a member of the organization (e.g., National Science Teachers Association) to be eligible?
5. Is the grant open to public (or private) school teachers at your grade level?
6. Do the demographics of your school match the priorities of the funding agent?
7. Can you carry out the proposal in the classroom or are other facilities required?
8. Are the funds outright or matching?
9. Can the project be replicated in the future?
10. Does the idea fall within district priorities?
11. Does the principal know about and approve of the proposal?

Also, if yours is a collaborative effort, consider whether or not your project will reach a large number of students. Try to expand the project so that it can be replicated in other classrooms of your grade level. Perhaps teams at other schools in your district can work with you collaboratively to implement a similar program. Or perhaps you can think in terms of a larger scale approach. With administrative participation in the planning process, you might expand the project to include community organizations and/or other school districts in your city, your state, or within your region of the United States. With some imagination, you may develop a large-scale project that has wide appeal. This will also expand the appeal of your project for the large-scale funder. Large foundations that fund unusual education projects that affect students in many regions of the country are listed in Resource D at the end of the book.

Guiding Questions in Writing the Proposal

Once you have identified potential funders and have listed application requirements for each grantmaker you will contact (and have answered the 10 preliminary questions), you have a good beginning. Next, you will want to contact some sources, perhaps by sending a letter of inquiry. Ask for the past year's annual report (if available) and the guidelines and priorities of the granting agency.

Carefully examine all published materials that you receive from each funding source that you have contacted. For each foundation to be contacted, you need to read application requirements in detail. Ask and answer another series of questions as you move into the next stages of your proposal development adventure.

1. Have you listed all information categories that are required by the foundation (for each grant application)?
2. Whom should you contact locally for help? Will a collaborative effort be helpful in obtaining the broad impact this project should have in solving a major problem? If so, which individual(s) or group(s) should you include?
3. Do you regularly have input from your colleagues on the project? Are they familiar with application guidelines? Do you regularly have an opportunity to discuss the proposal with them?
4. Is there an established inclusionary process to ensure the participation of important individuals and groups in the grantwriting process (administrators, central office staff, district subject specialists, media, etc.)?
5. What evidence does your group need to present to influence a potential funder about the importance of the program to the funder's mission?
6. Which specialists within the district have agreed to work with you on this project (e.g., to help with the evaluation design)?

7. Do you have a proposal planning calendar to assist in the completion of all pertinent details in a timely fashion?

Questions to Check on Completeness of the Proposal

A third set of general questions will help you in checking on the thoroughness of your completed proposal document. The following are examples of those check-off items. Throughout the book, we have included hints and tips to synthesize some key points.

1. Is the information in the proposal complete, as called for in the application guidelines?
2. Are data comprehensive in scope? In quantity? Do the data describe the challenges of the program to be funded? Have enough data been collected to describe the preprogram situation and to compare with ongoing program evaluations? Have itemizations been checked for accuracy?
3. Has the proposal presented ideas that represent the positions of each of the important stakeholders?
4. Does the proposal include program activities used successfully by "experts" in similar situations?
5. If working with a group, have specific roles been allocated for the project? Are expectations for these positions clear?
6. Does the proposal present a plan to broaden the funding base for this project and for continuation funding?
7. Does the proposal assure the funder that you have a financially sound base and that you will maximize their dollars? Have you identified funds received from other sources—newly discovered budgets, other grants, and in-kind contributions such as classroom volunteers? (See the Glossary for more about in-kind contributions.)

TIP: Proposals from successful applicants usually list one or more other funders! Go after several small gifts from your community members. Be entrepreneurial!

The reason for obtaining more than one source of funding is clear. As stated by one foundation director, "We are a small foundation.

Usually we can't entirely fund a project by ourselves. We look for partners in the funding process, and we expect applicants to obtain dollars from other funding partners also."

Other funding to support a proposed project and to list on a grant application can be from a variety of sources. Private sources of support might be gifts from philanthropists, parent groups, businesses, or other benefactors. One applicant to a foundation stated that the proposal was "under consideration" by another well-recognized foundation.

Characteristics of Successful Proposal Writers and Project Directors

Applicants who are willing to take risks and able to work cooperatively and creatively with others for solutions to problems within their classrooms and schools have the probability of obtaining greater levels of success in the grantwriting endeavor than do their counterparts. Most successful projects are highly collaborative and interactive activities, so skills of involvement, sharing, and mediation are important for success.

Three characteristics of successful grantseekers (and educational leaders in general) are that they are (a) risk takers, (b) mediators, and (c) "flexible"; that is, they approach the process from the vantage point that whatever is appropriate for the collaboration as a whole must also benefit all stakeholders in the program. The most effective proposal writer is thoroughly familiar with the funding process from a wide variety of vantage points and enjoys the role of mediator.

The ability to view each situation from other perspectives will enable the project director to share with other stakeholders responsibilities for all phases of project development. At least in some measure, the proposal should be designed to meet the primary requirements of each of the grantseeking parties *and* the mission of the funder. Stakeholders must feel that the project is important enough to warrant the development of a formal proposal, and each group needs to take some active role in the process. Roles can be assigned by the project initiator or some other administrator, or roles can be decided by the team using a consensus process. Whatever the leadership style of the person in charge, however, specific roles should be assigned for each group involved in the grant process as a way to build commitment to the project. Stakeholders who take ownership in the funding process may be able to generate additional support from numerous sources.

Through the grantwriting process, the individuals (or groups) who provide guidance in the development of the document assume a leadership role. Selection of the individual writer or of the writing team is uppermost for ensuring success in proposal development. The writer or writing team should be familiar with the school and district, with student problems in the community, and with positive and negative influences in the school setting that might affect completion of the funded project.

The Relationship Between the Proposal and the Project

The Proposal as a Contract

Funder purposes for proposals are stated on the grant application form. Accomplishment of the ultimate program goals and reduction or removal of the original need for the grant are the purposes for which a grant is awarded. The application form itself (often called the "boilerplate" by those people who write grants) becomes a part of the contract agreement with the funder to provide support for the project described. As the official document, therefore, a proposal needs to be specific and precise in content. It is a contract for services.

The application form process provides stipulations on which an award may be made and therefore constitutes a contractual arrangement between a grantee and grantor. A contractual agreement requires detailed information that contains a high level of accuracy based on the possible stringent legal scrutiny to which the contract may be held. Any changes in the agreement between you and your funder after the initial grant is made may change the contract or its implications. You may want to discuss the formal contract elements of the grant with a specialist.

Because budget and expenditure information will provide evidence of the funder's fiscal responsibility and may constitute the basis for the award of the grant, this information is crucial to the application. Accuracy, therefore, in collection and display of all budget data and in answering budget-related questions will help the funder know that monies will be appropriately allocated.

The Proposal as a Funding Instrument

Because a proposal is usually about money (funds), there will be considerable attention to fiscal issues in the proposal. Some details of fiscal responsibility and of funds budgeting need to be resolved early in the proposal development process.

The program development team should determine the process of budget oversight and expenditure prior to writing the proposal. A plan for implementing an appropriate grant oversight process and an individual or group designated as having formal fiscal accountability for the process are part of this effort. Oversight plans may (and usually do) vary substantially from one applicant to the next; they reflect differences in both programs and staffs. Funded proposals have one common theme, however: *The information requested by the funder is supplied in some detail.* Funded proposals

1. Request a specific amount of money.
2. Present a specific plan for expenditure of the funds.
3. Present a plan for oversight of the monies.

The well-designed and well-presented budget and fiscal responsibility plan should be presented to all important groups before the final proposal is written. Input from essential others, such as school board members, parent groups, and business partners, is important at this stage and may even elicit new dollars for the project. Throughout the proposal-writing process, you should be looking for additional funding sources.

When working collaboratively, *aggressively* look for new funding sources. Let your business partners know about your grant application and your need to provide evidence of support from other funding sources to increase your chances for obtaining funding. Your school board might reallocate dollars from other efforts to your project (possibly contingent on award of this grant); perhaps local corporations can provide in-kind contributions or donated goods, as well as needed dollars.

You will want to present information about how dollars from nonbudgeted funding sources might be allocated to support the project. The point here is to show the prospective funder that you have proactively widened the funding base for the project. You are demonstrating that you will not rely solely on the grantmaker to ensure the survival of your effort. This is key information for a funder who seeks to make as much impact as possible with limited dollars.

Funders seek to support long-lived changes in education. They seldom supply money for short-term solutions to long-range problems that do not affect the underlying, systemwide structure. And grants managers are developing greater sophistication in their approaches to gain external support for educational change. Several funders who previously limited awards to 1 year have begun multiyear grants to support projects that affect systemic change in the schoolwide organizations.

TIP: Funders want changes institutionalized in the system to ensure that improvements will outlast the grant dollars!

Don't make novice mistakes.

When asked about common errors of proposal writers, Kathryn Carey of the American Honda Foundation (AHF), responded:

Proposal writers make the error of *not believing our guidelines.* They think that, *despite what we say, we will fund projects;* for example, that we will fund engineering projects of all types (even though not within the guideline specifications). Do not assume, for example, that because we are a Japanese auto maker we will fund *any* Japan-related program. Read our application guidelines for specific information.

The wise grantseeker, having reviewed application materials published by a foundation, pays attention to interest statements of the funder. If you ignore this important point, you may well waste hours of work on a project that is not in keeping with the mission or interests of the funder.

TIP: Do not make incorrect assumptions about funder priorities and requirements. Correct information is a time-saver!

Positive Steps to a Successful Proposal

The successful grantseeker carefully examines all grant application guidelines published by the foundation. Although there is a wide range of funder requirements in the procedures to be followed in writing a grant application, the following basics are recommended for inclusion in an initial proposal:

1. Follow application guidelines. If there are no formal guidelines, check the foundation's annual report to review recent funded programs. For additional information, contact the foundation.
2. Present adequate evidence of the need for the program.
3. Obtain adequate budget information to meet guideline requests.
4. Include a 1-page budget summary with precise information.
5. Develop clear goals and present them succinctly.
6. Present an activities timeline.
7. Present an evaluation design.

Adhere to the basic requirements for grant applications. If the funder specifies information to be included in a budget and you do *not* have the information, contact someone who can assist you in obtaining it. *Include the requested information!*

TIP: *Fax questions you may have to the grants manager. Follow up with a call. Schedule an appointment for a phone interview.*

Information about awards made to other applicants, found in annual reports or through foundation collection libraries, can indicate a change in a grantmaker's focus. If you are unsure about funding priorities, ask the individual who is responsible for that foundation's grant awards. For example, when asked "What topics have you recently focused on (which are relatively new areas for program funding)?" Ms. Carey of the AHF responded, "Job training for youth and environmental education." When asked "What funding trends have become evident since you began your work with the foundation?" Ms. Carey replied, "[In my 10 years as Grants Manager for AHF,] the trend is now to fund projects for children at younger ages (pre-college versus higher education)"; and "the trend is toward funding multiyear versus 1-year projects in order to achieve systemic change!" Such information is available to guide an applicant in identifying funding possibilities.

TIP: Apply for grants from several funders! Try both private and public sources.

Before You Start Writing

Set aside a block of time for writing the proposal. Before writing begins, establish clear objectives for the project. If you are working with others in a collaborative project, set aside time to meet regularly with your colleagues. The success of your proposal may well depend on the selection of those with whom you will be working.

TIP: If collaborating on a proposal, select your teammates very carefully!

If possible, select as teammates individuals with whom you have already established working relationships. Successful teamwork requires that time be set aside for planning purposes on an ongoing basis. Include a planning schedule in your proposal.

Consider the funding process from a variety of vantage points. To help you develop a comprehensive overview of the process, combine the perspectives of each stakeholder, such as (a) the funder, (b) the grantwriter, (c) the teacher, (d) the student, (e) the administrator, (f) the school district, (g) the parent community, and (h) the business community. You need a grasp of the whole proposal plan and process *before you begin writing.*

Early "Preplanning" Saves Later Hassles

Before you start to work seriously, think deeply about the major issues that your project will address. This "preplanning" should result in an outline or set of notes to guide later work. Early in your work, it is helpful to

1. Identify and understand direct and indirect factors that influence your problem.

2. Identify possible solutions. If the project is a group effort, brainstorm as a team to get a set of good solutions.
3. Determine expected results and solutions.
4. Identify tasks that, when completed, will attain expected solutions.
5. Estimate total resources needed for the project.
6. Design and present a project evaluation plan.

Flexibility of Private Sources

The private sector of foundation and nonprofit support for education can provide a funding base for a whole range of programs that can be nontraditional or experimental. In contrast, publicly funded grants frequently support only programs that already have been established by the policy decisions of the agency. Foundation and other nonprofit organization types range from those with a philanthropic focus to those that conform to the specific requests of their principal donors. A foundation's annual report explains programming interests, awards made for the fiscal year, names of grant recipients, and award amounts. *Read the annual report. File it for reference purposes.*

Philanthropists have allocated many millions of foundation dollars to support a large number of new efforts to improve education. In the 1990s, these awards to education have focused on the attempt to overcome recognized problems in schools and are encouraged by U.S. tax law and the nonprofit status of foundations. Foundations have emphasized developing proficiency in the sciences and mathematics, providing models for overcoming problems of minority cultures, job training, and the teaching of new technologies, among other topics of major concern in the schools.

TIP: Be sure you have the most recent guidelines!

Foundation Support and Business Partnerships

Citizens are increasingly burdened with requests to fund new and expanded public programs through new taxes. School bond issues and increases in property taxes to pay for schools are being rejected, and foundation funding often provides the only source of growth capital and support for innovation in schools. The specification of a creative plan to fund your school or districtwide program requires that you do the preliminary work. But foundation funding is *not* a one-way street. Foundations work with educators to meet the needs of youth and the citizenry at large, as well as to benefit the corporate sponsor through good public relations and by providing extra (tax-exempt) benefits to employers by awarding some grants in areas where the corporate sponsor has many employees. Businesses, through school-business partnerships, provide often desperately needed goods and services, as well as dollars, to assist education. For example, businesses provide classroom volunteers and donate goods to schools to ensure that students receive special programs. Corporate giving programs are detailed in annual reports on file at libraries with foundation collections (see Resource C at the end of the book). These can be valuable resources on services to schools that are provided by businesses.

Search Strategies

INITIAL INFORMATION SEARCH

Successful models for solving a vast range of problems in education can be identified by a careful review of the research and literature, although the classroom practitioner or school administrator may not be thoroughly conversant with them. Before you spend many hours independently developing your idea, do an information search, such as through ERIC (Education Resources Information System), for recent projects that may be similar to the project you have in mind. If yours is a challenging idea that is not likely to have been attempted previously, do some careful sleuthing to see if your idea is really new. Historical information about your project idea should add to the dramatic impact of your request, but a truly new idea usually catches a funder's attention. If you are lucky enough to find some recent findings from experts who have completed similar projects, contact the individual or group for additional and up-to-date information. The fact that you have reviewed similar projects and their outcomes presents you as knowledgeable on what others have accomplished as related to your proposal for funding; it is another indicator of your meticulous attention to detail.

COLLABORATE TO REFINE THE PROBLEM

To find new models to resolve old, stagnant problems in education, you may need to review the problems with a renewed perspective. Look at the problem through someone else's eyes. Collaborative projects that might remove traditional barriers between educators, or between educators and other groups, would be well-received by grantmakers interested in educational reform. One strategy would be to plan with a group of colleagues; another is to involve other stakeholders as members of an advisory board. Develop project goals that will affect several schools, your entire school district, or several districts; expand your goals to include other groups, such as social service agencies or businesses.

TIP: *Show that you are familiar with work done by others in the field and that you can identify and cite trends in the research.*

WHAT DO FUNDERS LOOK FOR?

The grantmaker who is reading your proposal knows the corporate sponsor's goals and what the foundation wants to accomplish. The foundation's mission statement usually can be found in the foundation's annual report or grant guidelines. The grantmaker's mission is clearly stated in grant guidelines and should be a primary consideration for you as you select a particular funder to contact.

IDENTIFYING FUNDERS AND PLANNING TO APPLY

Private funders determine their funding priorities as they wish. This includes great diversity in the range of strategies used by grantmakers to identify projects they will support. Some foundations widely advertise available awards and grant deadlines in professional journals, grant publications, and news releases, whereas other funders request that no applicants submit proposals because applications are not open to the general public. Foundations also use their annual report to publicize the awarding of grants.

Occasionally, a foundation will specify that an applicant submit a 1-page prospectus (a letter of intent) summarizing the project. In this event, a funder may also stipulate that if the project interests the grantmaker, the applicant will receive an invitation to submit a full proposal.

Proposals for public funds are tightly controlled by mandate. Although there is some variation in the degree of control by agencies, there is generally more opportunity for flexibility in a privately funded project than in a public agency project. Therefore, a driving question in identifying funding sources is, Are you seeking private money or public money? If private, you can locate potential funders in community foundation offices, through university grants centers, libraries, and on-line with a computer modem. Education foundations, with incomes from philanthropic endowments, may provide exceptional, once-in-a-lifetime opportunities for the classroom teacher, administrator, and school district.

In Resource D, the authors have listed foundations that provide broad support to U.S. education. For each foundation, the following information is provided: grantmaker assets, dollars awarded, number of grants awarded, funding interests, whether an application form is required, and the name of the person to contact for information. Whenever possible, a phone number is also included.

Read your proposal as if you were the funder! Does your project, as presented, provide a new look at the problems? Provide data, both from your setting and from the literature, to support the funder's conclusion that yours is indeed a new perspective on an important issue. Link your project to large-scale goals such as *Goals 2000.* Stress the interrelationships between and among all elements of your project and the broader foundation or national goals. Emphasize and discuss the innovations in your proposal. When asked "What types of projects have recently interested you? What trends would you hope to see in the future?" Ms. Carey of the AHF answered, "I am looking for collaborations among colleges, universities, community colleges, high schools, elementary schools, school districts, *and* collaborations among funders."

Motivated by strong foundation support for their endeavors, education groups are learning to link with one another, as well as with other associated groups and agencies, to initiate long-overdue educational changes. One result is that strong and supportive working relationships are developing between and among groups that until recently had little contact.

ORGANIZATIONS AS RESOURCES

A good place to start searching for grants opportunities may be your own professional education associations. In addition to specialized grants that are offered through many education associations, an association may be an invaluable resource for current information on your proposal topic. Experts can be located and contacted to assist in providing background material for your proposal. A sample of professional education associations that you might contact is listed in Resource A at the end of the book. Enclosing a stamped, self-addressed envelope with your request for grant information from an organization may encourage a prompt response.

Some grants and awards to teachers, students, and school administrators that are offered by professional education associations are student incentive awards focused on minority students and dedicated to the mission of providing a support system to encourage the minority student to enter the teaching profession and to enable the student to remain in school.

Student incentive awards are intended as supplementary monies and are not huge sums. Generally, if you are seeking funding for all of a student's yearly college expenses, you should pursue several grants, awards, and scholarships simultaneously. However, check to be sure that there is no exclusionary provision in a grant award that precludes this approach.

WHY DO RESEARCH ON YOUR IDEA?

The time you spend doing basic research on your idea should serve you well. You need to know what has been accomplished by others so that you can contact experts for additional information to guide your process. You need to build upon their successes and try to avoid any pitfalls that they encountered.

Use on-line information databases or review other research on your idea at a convenient research library. Seek pertinent models for solution strategies that have worked to remedy problems similar to yours, both in schools and in classrooms.

You may want to know the locale of the closest library housing a good foundation collection. Libraries with complete foundation resource collections are listed in Resource C at the end of the book.

Once you have a list of solution possibilities that you can cite to support your proposal, develop your own creative ideas on the base of earlier work. Your design should reflect your expertise on the project subject.

Submission Steps

The review process differs substantially from one funder to another, and this may influence how you make contact with the foundation. Large corporations may rely on consultants or staff to review proposals, whereas smaller funders may rely on an individual, family members, or board members to perform the review and make the funding decision. A review of foundations listed in *The Foundation Directory* (Foundation Center, 1993a, 1995) reveals some with more than 30 employees, whereas others have no full-time staff. Small family foundations frequently request that an applicant submit a proposal to the foundation president (often a family member). Because staffs vary in size and capability in terms of looking at large numbers of proposals, there are differing procedures in place at foundation offices to handle the volume of proposals submitted.

PRELIMINARY APPLICATIONS

Ask about the specific process required by that funder. Some reviewers request submission of a preliminary application that is shorter than a full-length proposal.

Once the initial reviewer determines that you have an appropriate project to submit to the board for approval, you may be asked to present a formal proposal to the board of directors. At that time, you may be asked additional questions about your project. Review the board membership, and then consider that information to help you prepare material designed to influence the review board positively.

Sourcebooks that have compilations of education funders are listed in the bibliography. Develop a list of several funders with correct names, addresses, and phone numbers. Call to verify names and official titles *before* submitting your proposal. Ask and answer this question: Does the individual designated as grants administrator in your information still hold that position? There is some turnover in grant administration staffs. Call potential funders to check uncertain information. If you are unsure about the spelling of a director's name, call and ask.

Never use old guidelines; no doubt there have been changes over time in funding priorities. Obtain the most recent guidelines directly from the funder. Although there are similarities among foundations, all grantmakers are not alike. Some funding organizations distribute guidelines and have specific submission deadlines; other funders have *no* guidelines and accept proposals continuously throughout the year. Commonly, however, proposals are accepted only once or twice per year. Requirements vary widely, and you must decide how to meet the specific demands of each funder.

QUERY LETTERS

If, after checking available information, you remain uncertain about a funder's requirements, a query letter to the funder may be indicated. Query letters also can be required by a funder as an ongoing part of the application process. Check the specific requirements of the funding source. *The Foundation Directory* (Foundation Center, 1993a, 1995), among other resources, provides such information.

LETTERS OF INTENT

One way funders can simplify the process is to request that a complete proposal not be submitted at the outset. The funders may request instead that you submit only a letter of intent and an outline of your idea. Guidelines usually spell out clearly what is to be included in the letter of intent, including deadlines for letters of intent serving as preliminary screening instruments. Other funders accept letters of intent on an ongoing basis. These are like the query letter or a letter of inquiry. They help grant administrators in eliminating or making a case for proposed projects and are most effective when they "grab" the reader and elicit emotional responses. An effective letter of intent is one that immediately generates a positive reaction from the reader.

Remember that in cases where the grant administrator may see only one item, that is, your letter of intent, you have only one chance to make an impact: First impressions count. Make the most of this opportunity through the use of selected vocabulary to draw a "visual description" of the impact your program will have on, for example, students and their families. Consider the credibility and impact of visual materials. Use letterhead stationary, other visuals, or a short videotape or audiotape to introduce yourself. Supplemental materials can be helpful in the right situation; so can a handwritten letter. Attach a strong resumé to the letter of intent and letters from important individuals known to the funder. Stay within the page or word limits. Write in the active voice. Avoid jargon. Persuade the reviewer that your idea is very worthy!

Some funders do not like to receive letters of intent. A program administrator of a major education foundation clearly stated in a recent conversation that she would not consider a letter of intent prior to submission of a proposal. Indeed! She indicated that she would be irritated by the lack of the inquirer's consideration of expressed proposal guidelines, which she expected to be followed by the grant writer "to the letter." Instead, this funder requested that applicants enclose a cover letter that outlines and summarizes the proposal. Be sure that you follow the preferences of the individual funder. Make a phone call before you send a letter of intent. *A reminder: Check to see what projects have been funded in the past.* Awards are listed in each foundation's annual report. Award information is also available at grant libraries.

Writing a Cover Letter

Guidelines

Assure the funder at the initial screening stage that there is a strong link between the project's goals and the funder's mission. Your cover letter, similar to an abstract of main points, will help you link your idea to a foundation's priorities, which are listed in the annual report that identifies current grantees and award amounts. Annual reports are available on several CD-ROM databases (Moody's and Compact Disclosure are two of these), and they can be reviewed at designated foundation libraries. Addresses and phone numbers of foundation libraries are provided in Resource C at the end of the book. Call for hours of operation before visiting a library!

In a survey of 164 foundations providing funding for human services, Coley and Scheinberg (1990) found that 78% required a cover letter from applicants, and 73% required submission of a standard proposal. You may well decide to include both a cover letter and the standard proposal in your submission. Although a funder may not specify that a cover letter be included, such a letter is a method of introducing the proposal to the grantmaker (and piquing interest).

Tips From a Successful Grantseeker

Fern Aefsky, an administrator in the Monticello, New York, Central School District, has developed many successful proposals. The following are some of her hints to first-time proposal writers for receiving grant money.

Private foundation grants encompass a large variety of funding sources. When searching for funding, these suggestions will help you match your need to dollars available.

Resources in almost every library catalog private foundations. Read the description to see if the mission of the foundation supports your mission for funding. Write to all that appear to meet this criterion, and carefully read the information explaining the submission of proposals for funding.

An immediate goal is to ascertain whether the fund amount is enough to support your idea and worth the time it takes to complete the required proposal. Proposal development is time consuming, and each funding source requires specific information presented in a specific way. You must follow directions exactly if you expect a foundation to review your proposal.

When submitting a proposal, ensure that the language in your request matches the wording in the mission statement of the foundation. Timelines must be followed, including the number of copies, cover letter directions, and submission dates. Be aware that the dates for the funding differ from deadline dates, and care must be taken to write the correct project dates in the proposal. These seemingly minor facts can take your request out of the running for dollars!

Qualifying for large amounts of money is difficult when beginning a search for funding. Foundations that provide large sources of money look for prior substantial dollars of support for a project. This information is requested for most proposal submissions.

Ask the foundation for additional information. A key question is the percentage of requests funded. Try to ascertain which programs are receiving the strongest support. The secretary or administrative assistant listed as a contact can provide useful information.

Local sources of revenue dollars are available for educational purposes. Service organizations such as Kiwanis, Rotary, and Knights of Pythias clubs have local and state grants for specified purposes. If funding of $2,500 or less is requested from two or three sources, the time spent on requesting funds from these sources is well-spent. Typically, you can make a presentation to the club. Local clubs like to fund local projects, and this paves the way for state dollars from the club becoming available.

Large companies (IBM, Xerox, insurance companies, etc.) usually have community outreach programs. A presentation to this committee can lead to funding because the local community is the focus of these groups, who can then tap into larger funding pools of their organization.

Once funds are granted, use the information to apply for larger grants. These data help build the trust of foundation programs because other funding enables foundation boards to see that money will be spent on purposeful programs, supported by people other than program directors.

Once funds are received, it is imperative that you keep careful records. You must keep track of when reports (quarterly or yearly updates) are due, of submission deadlines for continued funding, and how funds were spent. Each funding source has specific criteria to be included in reports, and the protocol must be followed exactly as written.

Funds are available from many sources. Match your needs with those of the foundation. First, apply locally for funds, and use small grant amounts to help gain larger grant funds. Record management is vital to continued funding. Establish a relationship by mail and telephone with key personnel from the agency, so that these people will assist you in bridging the foundation's goals and your personal goal in obtaining funds.

Summary

If you have good ideas, you may need help and support to get them started. External support, in the form of funding and cooperative efforts of other groups, may be the route that you would like to take. The development of proposals for funding support and the formulation of partnerships and collaboratives are ways that you may expand your impact. It is hard work, but it is fun. The rest of this book will offer specifics on how to start and succeed in this challenging arena.

TIP: *Be aggressive in your search for new and supportive dollars! Let others know that you need their assistance!*

2

Funding Strategies and School/Business Partnerships

Chapter Highlights

- Donor Research (Where to Look)
- Ideas to Enlist a Funder's Support
- The Selection Process
- Some Success Stories
- Partnerships to Expand Your Impact

Chapter 1 provided an overview of the funding process and discussed initial steps to identify a potential funder (or funders) for your project. It included information about developing and writing effective query letters, letters of intent, and cover letters; tips from a successful proposal writer also were offered.

Chapter 2 offers more information about effective donor research and insights into how to match your goals to the funder's interests. Important sources of funding are identified, and ideas to help you catch the interest of a funder to obtain support for your project are provided in this chapter. Some success stories are included as models, illustrating the fact that many ingenious approaches are available to you. Your creativity in this endeavor is the key. Chapter 2 provides considerable information on collaboration and partnerships as ways to increase your organization's impact.

Researching Possible Donors

Seeking sources of funding support is an important task. Those who are successful at obtaining grants approach this task as a science—by doing careful donor research. Donor research is the *entire process* of identifying a range of potential funding sources to support your idea. There are numerous ways to approach this task.

Published documents, such as *Grants for Elementary and Secondary Education* (Foundation Center, 1993c), *The Annual Register of Grant Support* (Foundation Center, 1994a), and *Foundation Reporter 1995* (The Taft Group, 1994), may be very helpful at the beginning of your quest. *The Foundation Directory* (Foundation Center, 1993a, 1995), for example, lists the foundations by state and provides such information as purposes, grant preferences, dates in the award cycle, size and number of projects funded, persons on the board of directors, and contact details (name, address, and phone number).

Check reference materials in the bibliography for additional resources. Note in this regard that some foundations have shifted the focus of their grant awards to public education in recent years. Be sure the foundation or corporate grant guidelines for education grants you use are up-to-date.

Databases such as DIALOG and CompuServe are available to help you with the search. If you have a computer, tap into on-line databases. The Foundation Center, for example, has current and updated data available through DIALOG Information Services and other on-line utilities. If you are affiliated with a university library or have access to the Internet (you will need a computer modem), you are ready to begin. Information that may be obtained in a search of the Foundation Center's databases includes

1. Type of education project supported by the foundation as well as the type of project that the foundation does *not* fund.
2. Whether or not the general public may apply.
3. The names, addresses, contact persons, and phone numbers at each foundation, including names of officers and trustees. You may even know some of these people, so

check to see if you have a personal contact on a board. It may be helpful to speak with someone who has additional information about a foundation.

4. Process for application, whether or not proposal guidelines are available on request, and availability of an annual report.

5. A listing of foundations that support education in each of the states.

Word-of-mouth information about funding opportunities is particularly powerful but usually not easily available until after you have received at least one grant and have become part of the network of funded projects. People who run projects often have the "inside track" to funding sources.

Professional organizations may have persons on staff who can steer you toward potential funders. The organization may know of projects similar to yours that already are being supported. Ask questions at meetings and conferences to find out who or what agency might be interested in helping you with your idea.

Attend one or more good proposal-writing and grant-exploring seminars. These are held in central locations and are often sponsored by professional organizations and firms that specialize in knowing about external funding processes.

First Impressions Count

Part of your donor research is planning your first contact with the funding source. Here, as in many other situations, first impressions are important.

Why is face-to-face contact with the funder important? Everyone (even the funder) is human! Later in the funding process, the proposal reader should be able to link a face and a personality to the name on the proposal. One highly successful proposal-writer colleague who attended a seminar on the funding process described the response of a program officer at a major education foundation to the question, "How do you screen proposals?" The response was, "I place proposals in two piles—those from people I know and those from names I do not recognize." The implication was that only proposals from recognized sources would get even a cursory peek, because this individual was overloaded with a glut of submissions.

This is surely an exaggeration of the case, but do consider making the requisite contacts with the appropriate funding official(s) ahead of time. If you have done an effective job of laying the groundwork and preparing the funder to accept and read your idea, the official at the funding agency will

1. Remember the initial contact and, more important, remember *you.*
2. Place your proposal in the "good" pile to be read.
3. Select your proposal for funding.

By doing some careful preparatory work, you will have a more reasonable expectation of passing the initial screening stage *and* having the opportunity to get funding for your proposal.

THE MYTH ABOUT "KNOWING SOMEONE"

Ms. Kathryn Carey, Grants Manager for the American Honda Foundation (AHF), dispels the myth that you must know someone at the foundation to get your idea supported. She says that the "inside information" concept for marketing a proposal to a funder is incorrect: "AHF does not care how many Hondas you own, or how many board members you know." The important selection criteria are presented in the mission statement and grant application guidelines, and foundation personnel expect all prospective recipients to follow these carefully. Printed information about program officials or program directors who are responsible for selection of grantees may be out-of-date. Circumvent lack of up-to-date written information about important contact persons by checking names by telephone ahead of time.

When you meet with your face-to-face contact, obtain as much information as you can about the funding process itself. Develop and implement your presentation plan as per the unique process of that particular funder. For example, if the proposal selection is made by one primary individual, not by committee, attempt to establish dialogue with that person and then to nurture that particular relationship. On the other hand, if a committee is charged with the selection process, you will want to know more about each committee member instrumental in the selection process. You should attempt to make face-to-face contact with each of those individuals prior to submitting your proposal to the screening process.

Budget constraints in your school or district may prevent you from traveling to the foundation offices for such meetings. Don't let this discourage you from seeking grants! Most grants are awarded on the basis of the proposal alone. If you wish to "meet" the grants manager through a telephone call, you may thus ensure some name recognition at the time your application is reviewed.

Ideas to Enlist Funders' Support

FIND A PHILANTHROPIST WHO CARES!

The senior author once had the great pleasure of a personal meeting with the development director for a college of education at a major university. Over a period of years, this master grantseeker had demonstrated his expertise. His ideas for donor contact and his ability to motivate donors to become involved in the college's projects, along with his careful stewardship of donors over many months—sometimes years—combined to prove enormously effective to the college in obtaining support from private individuals and from private foundations. He had obtained millions of dollars in support for the institution during his tenure. His approach of designing an individualized plan can be used successfully by all grantseekers. The most effective aspect of the process is the grants plan that is custom tailored to the particular interests of the individual philanthropist. Donor research provides the key to this process. The plan is built upon careful research into the interests of each major entrepreneur and identification of potential or proven philanthropists in the area. Bibliographic sources, a visit to a library that has a good foundation collection, and careful reading of annual reports, most of which are now available on-line, will assist you in the process.

Delineate in your plan short-term and long-range goals both for your project and for your organization. Just as important are the designated processes through which you will stay in touch to keep this philanthropist and funder up-to-date on what is happening that would be of interest to him or her.

Over time, moreover, the funder's familiarity with your credentials and basic trust in you personally as the project director will increase. The philanthropist will become involved in your project as a stakeholder, and your chances of receiving project funding will become significantly heightened. Long term, the philanthropist you have targeted will trust in your ability to deliver what you say you will accomplish. How so? Demonstrate your acumen and your budget astuteness. Summarize for this person the small grants you have received from other sources that affect this project. Provide examples that illustrate your ability as a communicator (perhaps a school, districtwide, or collaborative newsletter that includes information about one of your projects).

It is conceivable that a philanthropist may not initially respond to your letter of request or invitation. However, after a period of time, once personal contact has been established, a method usually can be found that works in generating interest (assuming that you have done a proficient job of linking this person to your project).

POINTERS

When you submit a personal letter to assess a person's or foundation's actual interest in your endeavor, you might invite the person to visit your school or school district to see a particular project in the person's area of interest. Consider a luncheon or other social function in which those constituents who support your proposed project would be involved (e.g., administrators, teachers, or school board members from neighboring schools or school districts with similar programs). If yours is to be a collaborative effort, discuss with your partners an orchestrated plan for working with the philanthropist to achieve mutual goals. This collaboration could provide a strong funding base for your new programs and future funding efforts.

All approaches to a funder should be modified for the specific funder! This includes writing and modifying the proposal, making direct person-to-person contact with the funder, and developing a plan to communicate with the funder on an ongoing basis. The goal is the funder's initial and sustained support of your project over time.

Once you have reviewed a substantial number of possible grant-makers and have identified at least two or three potential funders for your project, decide how will you introduce yourself to these two or three key individuals.

TIP: *Make face-to-face contact with the funder if possible. If not, use phone and written contact processes skillfully.*

IDEAS TO DEVELOP NAME RECOGNITION WITH FUNDERS

1. Remember that some major funding programs have a local focus. Try to identify funding programs that are in your region of the country, your state, or your city if at all possible.
2. Be certain that you have correctly linked program purposes to your project's goals.
3. Be certain that you know the correct name of the funding agency and the primary funding official.
4. Do your homework. Find out which organizations this individual or his or her foundation support. Attend meetings held by these groups that are open to the public.
5. Review stationery letterhead for names of board members or board of trustees.
6. Devise informal methods of networking to make yourself known to one or more of the foundation board members or trustees.

A SUMMARY OF THE PROCESS

1. Identify a philanthropist or foundation interested in your type of project.
2. Develop a comprehensive and individualized plan to interest this person.
3. Design a short-term strategy and a long-range plan for support.
4. Make personal contact with the funder.
5. Devise a plan to enlist support of key others.
6. Send a letter of inquiry and interest.
7. Submit the required proposal.
8. Establish ongoing dialogue with the funder.
9. Steward the funder through various phases of your project to ensure that the funder becomes a stakeholder.

Now you have taken a proactive stance to set the groundwork for reception of your proposal. *Remember, someone must read your proposal before it can be selected for funding!*

Finding Noncompetitive Support

A Publisher's Story

The acquisitions editor of a professional publisher informed the senior author that although the company does not have grant guidelines available, nor does it publicize grants it has made to education, company leaders are genuinely interested in education projects. As it happens, a clever grantseeker (one who had obviously done her homework) contacted this publisher, requesting (and receiving) funding for an education project that was directly on target with this publisher's mission.

So, despite the fact that this publisher was not listed as a funder, and no literature was available to indicate that the publisher was a prospective funder, a rather large grant was awarded to this educator. (This person did not even have an inside track!)

Jefferson Davis Primary School and D. C. Heath

Dr. Lula Mae Perry is Principal of the Jefferson Davis Primary School in Hazelhurst, Georgia. One of Dr. Perry's major accomplishments was that she was able to obtain the support of a textbook publisher, D. C. Heath. In fact, she acquired the entire series of new 1994 math textbooks, *Connections*, from Heath by "simply picking up the phone and asking." Dr. Perry was introducing a new mathematics curriculum into her classrooms at the time she requested texts from Heath. The response from Heath, however, was far greater than expected. Each classroom was supplied with this innovative math text. To Dr. Perry's credit, she achieved outstanding results in the use of these new texts. Her success in implementing an innovative new math curriculum resulted in higher math test scores in her school, as contrasted with other schools both statewide and nationally. Her documented success in using the donated texts resulted in her school's designation as a laboratory school for a forthcoming text to be published by D. C. Heath.

Dr. Perry received her initial bequest from D. C. Heath without submitting a formal grant request. She obtained a commitment worth many dollars to her school simply by calling the publisher directly! Can this approach work for you? Perhaps, but certainly not every time. Even if this particular method does not work, there are numerous alternatives to writing a formal proposal. Educators have access to many sources of support. Certainly, a formal written proposal is not the only approach to obtaining support for your school or classroom. Do you have parents in your classroom who have made substantial contributions in the past? Can these folks be relied on to enlist the support of other parents for your project? If parents are unable to contribute monies to your project, can they be relied on to donate their services, or can they make contributions of goods from their small businesses? If you ask, remember that reciprocity is fair: Don't ask local businesses for support and then do all of your shopping at Wal-Mart!

Orlando, Florida, and the Rosen Foundation

A LONG-RANGE COMMITMENT

In Orlando, Florida, a prominent hotelier, Harris Rosen, has taken a personal interest in redevelopment of the community in which his hotel is located. In response to his concern about problems of children and families in this area, Mr. Rosen donated $50,000 seed money to start a program offering guaranteed education from ages 2 to 22 to children in an inner-city neighborhood. The first step in the commitment, made in Phase 1 of the donation, provided for preschool classes for children ages 2 to 4, and vocational and child-rearing classes for their parents in Tangelo Park. Harris Rosen's contribution has enabled the Tangelo Park Elementary School to expand its preschool efforts and open a Family Service Center. Later, the program will fill in gaps in federal Head Start programs and other services for preschoolers.

During several months of talks with educators, the philanthropist said that they had decided that they had to reach very young children to start. In preschool, a safe and healthy environment and meals and bonding opportunities would be provided. Parents would learn parenting skills and take vocational education.

Over the past decade, the Rosen Foundation has provided hundreds of young people with scholarships to colleges and universities. The plan for Tangelo Park is that as children continue through grade school and high school, mentor projects will be offered through the private sector: summer camp, outings, picnics, and other opportunities. Each child who graduates from high school will have a guarantee of college. The idea is to take a deprived neighborhood and turn it into "an advantaged neighborhood," said Mr. Rosen. "These kids are as capable as any other kids; they just have not had the opportunities. If they work hard and stay in school, they can go to college." Mr. Rosen hopes that the program becomes contagious, and that within the next decade, every inner city has a plan modeled on Tangelo Park with a corporation, endowment, foundation, or philanthropist backing it. "We're not asking for federal or state funds," he said. "We'll do it ourselves."

Sarah Sprinkel, the early childhood program specialist for the Orlando Public School District, is the person who made first contact with the funder. She has also successfully managed the grant over time. Most effective is the personal rapport she has established with the funder to ensure the project's long-term success. In effect, she has become the "sole grantee" for this project.

RAMIFICATIONS OF BEING THE SOLE GRANTEE

Naturally, the first consequence of import as the sole grantee is the immediate (or prompt) elimination of many potential competitors for grant dollars. If you have earmarked a funder that does not widely advertise or market the availability of funds, you are ahead of the game. And if you can establish a personal contact with the funder, you are definitely on the right track.

Developing School/Business Partnerships

School/business partnerships help people seeking project funding in at least three ways.

1. Partnerships enlist the assistance of many more individuals and groups in your endeavors through the development

of a wider support base for your project. Potential opposition to your effort likely will be reduced or eliminated.
2. Operating expenses incurred by partnerships can be covered.
3. Dollars to ensure ongoing support of partnership projects may be generated for schools and businesses.

Developing Partnerships With Business: North Montco Technical Career Center

Jim Kraft, Assistant Director of the North Montco Technical Career Center in Lansdale, Pennsylvania, has developed effective partnerships with his school's business community for the past 7 years. Dr. Kraft believes that the most effective first contact with a business to be enlisted as a potential school partner is one made in person, not via mail! He provides the following guidelines to the process.

North Montco Technical Career Center has established a close working relationship with local business and industry. As in some public vocational training facilities, successful business and education partnerships frequently are a means of survival for small businesses, especially in hard economic times. Many small businesses depend on business and education working together to help them compete with big business and foreign competition.

The partnership relationship has grown out of a community-based need for training or retraining the workforce as technology evolves. Businesses also want to do their part to provide opportunities for the future workforce. Unlike many academic-track students, 95% of the North Montco graduates will reside in the area after graduation. This means a greater commitment on the part of new and existing partnerships—to use a colloquial term, "more bang for the buck." The return on the businesses' investment in the center is quite high.

Contacts are made through a network of business interaction. The school is active with the chamber of commerce and with many small businesses that provide curriculum input and work experience for the students. Technical schools also reap the benefits of developing partnerships through a variety of means. The following is a list of some ways that North Montco educators and local industry personnel work together.

TIME

- Provision of industry training opportunities for teachers (e.g., a summer clinic to become updated with latest technology)
- Opportunity to serve on various committees: occupational advisory, strategic planning, tech prep, youth apprenticeship, school marketing, and so on

MONETARY

- Scholarships
- Awards
- Donated equipment and materials
- Defrayal of operating expenses (e.g., yearbook sponsor, printing, school plays, and school videos)

EDUCATION

- Mentoring, youth apprenticeship programs
- Job-site work experience
- Internships or job shadowing
- Interviews for class projects
- Judges for student competitions

OTHER

- Marketing of the school's programs
- Guest speakers on industry-related topics

One successful North Montco partnership endeavor occurred in the early 1990s. Spring Garden College in Philadelphia closed its doors, and local pharmaceutical companies from suburban Philadelphia became concerned about where they could send their employees to be trained to become packaging equipment mechanics. After discussing this concern with the North Montco administration, three pharmaceutical companies—Merck Pharmaceutical Manufacturing Division, Rhone-Poulenc-Rorer Pharmaceutical Incorporated, and McNeil Consumer Products Company—formed a partnership with North Montco Technical Career Center to develop a customized curriculum to train the employees at the career center. The companies donated training equipment, time to install the equipment, and time to train the trainer. In return, North Montco built a new lab in which to house the equipment and conduct the training. This partnership not only benefits the pharmaceutical companies but also provides an industry environment for secondary students to be trained to enter the workforce. Spinoffs to this partnership involved training agreements with additional local businesses and certification recognition through the Packaging Mechanics Association of America.

LINKING BUSINESS AND INDUSTRY TO THE EDUCATION CURRICULUM

North Montco uses an occupational advisory committee to oversee the technical relevance of the curriculum. This committee also provides equipment purchase recommendations and facility modification recommendations.

The tech prep (technical preparatory) initiative is another example of how business and education form partnerships to benefit all participants. Tech prep was coined by Dale Parnell (1985) in *The Neglected Majority* as a program that addresses the middle 50% of high-school-age students who do not go on to college or do not complete a college course of study.

Tech prep involves a collaborative effort between high schools, vocational-technical schools, and postsecondary institutions offering a technical course of study. The key is for industry to be a part of the process to ensure that a technical skill-oriented, relevant curriculum is intact. One means to accomplish this goal is to use the Developing A Curriculum (DACUM) process, which involves people from business, high schools, and postsecondary institutions. The process begins with occupational analysis, moves through program planning, and concludes with instructional design. The three components— DACUM chart development, curriculum planning, and instructional development—in combination, enable educators and businesspeople to design an academic or technical skill program based on the reality of the workplace.

Another success story in many of the states is the youth apprenticeship program concept. Designed after the European model of youth apprenticeship, students combine their high school academic curriculum with technical training, both in a school environment and in industry. This program is a tripartite effort between the Department of Labor, the Department of Commerce, and the Department of Education. Unlike traditional academic and technical training, the sponsoring industry has a vested interest in what is taught and how it is taught. Students are trained under a mentor; upon graduation from high school, apprentices may qualify for advanced standing in an adult apprenticeship program or a tech prep associate degree program, or go directly into the workforce.

HOW TO BEGIN BUILDING A PARTNERSHIP

The first step is to develop a list of your needs. A brainstorming session with representatives from your school works quite well. Also determine the geographic boundaries for your project; let your project have a presence in a defined area. Most educators will initially identify businesses within their school district or county.

Second, identify the businesses you want to approach. Your local chamber of commerce is a good starting point to get your prospective partners identified. The chamber can supply a listing of businesses and contact people, and perhaps even provide a database that you can use to narrow or broaden your list. Other options might be to contact your state department of commerce and your state department of education.

Third, determine your strategy for approaching the companies. Companies are usually asked to sponsor many nonprofit organizations or to donate to other good causes over the course of the year. They will need to see the benefit of developing the partnership that you are proposing. *Do not use the mail to express your intent!* Personal contact works best. If you have a long list of potential partners, divide your list and make personal contacts. Call before visiting, but do not divulge all details of your intent over the phone. State that you are a representative of the school and you would like to foster a closer working relationship with the business.

Fourth, be prepared for your visit. Do your homework and discover basic information about the business before visiting (e.g., approximate number of employees and product line). A handout outlining the successes of the school with other partnership options will prove beneficial. Attach your business card or a contact's name, address, and telephone number to the handout. Do not do all of the talking. Allow the partnership to begin at this point. Make sure you describe the next step. The partnership will go nowhere without swift follow-up.

Fifth, send a personalized letter thanking the person for investing valuable time. Emphasize the importance of the partnership and that you are interested in working together in the future.

IMPACT OF PARTNERSHIPS

To determine the impact of business and education partnerships, statistics and the qualitative judgment of satisfying the predetermined goals are the best indicators. Examine the image of the partnerships in the community. Look at the numbers of students served and the businesses that have benefited from the collaborative efforts. A survey of the participants and observers can yield useful data.

From a technical center viewpoint, the final product is a better trained workforce. Industry can provide the caliber of training that the school environment can only simulate. Real-world experiences benefit all students.

Postsecondary schools also can be the beneficiaries of business partnerships, either by receiving students who have been a part of the secondary education partnerships or through developing their own partnerships. The curriculum at the college level can be validated through input from the businesses who will be hiring college graduates. The process for becoming involved in partnerships at the postsecondary level parallels the process described for the elementary and secondary school environments.

A major impact will be that business and education partnerships are self-perpetuating. Much media attention is focused on the schools and their standing in the community. Businesses will want to be a part of the action. Superintendents, in turn, will have a vested interest in the success of the partnership concept. The expansion of activities provided in good partnerships has a dollar value. In a way, this added support is its own successful "project" of equal value to a successful proposal for funds.

TIPS FOR A SUCCESSFUL PARTNERSHIP

- Use and publicize the business suggestions that are pertinent.
- Communicate with the business frequently.
- Make business partners part of the decision-making process.
- Give the business recognition (e.g., Chamber of Commerce meetings, newspaper articles, etc.).
- Spotlight and thank the business whenever possible.
- Allow the business to educate the educators (e.g., schedule a Business and Education Day).
- Include the business in school activities (e.g., as guest speakers in curriculum development or as guests at events).

TIPS ON WHAT TO AVOID

Maintaining a positive give-and-take relationship cannot be emphasized enough. Educators seeking monetary support must approach the business with the idea of a joint project having benefits for both the company and the school. Avoid overuse of business for educational endeavors; too much of a good thing may result in participation burnout. Be concerned about the number of committee meetings and the need to have action items. Michael Snyder, School-to-Work Opportunities Coordinator at the Pennsylvania Department of Education, offers two further tips:

1. The primary thing we do wrong as educators is to approach businesses by asking how we can serve their needs. We need to take the time to clarify our intentions; an outline is an excellent tool. Another problem is that we frequently approach the CEO when we should be speaking with a business administrator who can be more beneficial to the organization.
2. When the economy is on the upswing, business leaders are eager to assist the local school personnel with monetary resources. When the economy is poor, business leaders turn to the vocational school for training assistance. During the early 1990s, when businesses were laying off employees, the vocational school remained busy retraining

the remaining workforce to be multiskilled. This is an example of the give-and-take relationship between business and education.

Proof that telephone calls do not work as well as personal visits to the companies are the letters of support sent to businesses when the youth apprenticeship program at North Montco was securing industry support. Out of 50 letters sent, representatives from only one company responded to the mailing, whereas 14 of the original 50 businesses contacted through personal visits by school staff were enlisted to become involved by sponsoring students.

The concept of business and education partnerships is not new but can be described as an untapped viable resource available to all willing participants. The risk is not great if all participants share a common vision. According to Marsha Hurda, Adult Education Coordinator at North Montco Technical Career Center, "Roadblocks are not viewed as failures." Developing partnerships will not always yield immediate anticipated results, but like many activities in life, much can be gained from the partnership process. The efforts will be worthwhile.

State Offices of Business and Citizen Partnerships

Many states have allocated resources and developed networks to support school/business partnerships. The Florida Office of Business and Citizen Partnerships is a statewide information network that provides educators with partnership information and information on training and programs to increase family involvement. A family resource directory and a parent primer were developed to create interest in Florida's *Blueprint 2000* for education goals. Families are involved in the School Advisory Council (SAC), parent workshops, and training programs. Together with community involvement coordinators, schools, community organizations, and businesses are working for school improvement as part of the legislative mandate to assist the state in reaching *Blueprint 2000* goals. Florida's Department of Education (DOE) has developed a comprehensive training package for community involvement. Twenty-five hundred chairpersons of SACs throughout the state actively participate in the state's School/Business Partnership Conference.

A sampling of Florida's partnerships reveals that the following classroom enrichment programs are partially supported by businesses with both dollars and in-kind goods and services.

- Math Superstars is a math enrichment program managed by volunteer business partners to help elementary and middle school students enhance their mathematics skills.
- Networks is a volunteer-managed, after-school academic enrichment program with hands-on activities in math, science, social studies, language arts, computers, and personal fitness (K-8).
- Peer Cross Tutors pairs older students as tutors for younger students.
- Project Home Safe uses volunteers to teach third through fifth graders to be safe when they are home alone through self-esteem, safety, and nutrition lessons.
- Rockin' Readers are senior adult readers who assist prekindergarten through second graders in developing reading readiness skills, self-esteem, and emotional maturity.
- SuperScientists are volunteers who are trained to conduct simple science experiments in elementary classrooms.
- Intergenerational Programs pairs senior adults with students to serve as tutors, mentors, readers, and classroom helpers and conducts a variety of other programs.
- Wee Care provides activities, strategies, and training for volunteers who assist in prekindergarten.
- Youth Motivators matches students and community and business volunteers with at-risk students. Motivators are committed to helping students better their lives academically, socially, and mentally while assisting them to set and reach goals toward graduation.

Contact your state department of education to identify existing school/business partnerships in your region. Contact stakeholders in successful partnerships to obtain additional suggestions for building your own school partnerships with businesses. Ask these individuals to identify other businesses that may be interested in partnership participation. Use a computer network (Internet, etc.), contact your local business organizations (including chambers of commerce), or call your state or local agency to get assistance in generating a list of possible partners for your endeavor.

Florida Commissioner of Education's Business Recognition Award

The commissioner's Business Recognition Award is presented annually to recognize exemplary programs in each of the five Department of Education regions within the state of Florida. Partnerships with statewide impact are also recognized.

An example of an effective partnership is the working relationship between Optical Data Corporation and Sunrise Middle School in which Optical Data has provided laser disc equipment and educational programs that students use to study social studies, math, and science. An important feature is Optical Data's contribution of trainers to teach the teachers how to use the equipment.

Commenting on Optical Data's partnership with Sunrise Middle School, where she is a technical specialist, Mary Baker said,

> It's not just that they send this stuff to us and say, Good luck. . . . Just throwing money at a school won't help. It's like giving you a Jaguar that's a stick shift that you don't know how to use. Businesses and schools need to walk hand-in-hand.

Judy Meyer, Director of Florida Department of Education's Office of Business and Citizen Partnerships, indicates that business leaders who once thought a $10,000 donation was the key to school improvement are "now discussing magnet programs, flexible scheduling, and cooperative learning." In 1993-1994, businesses contributed almost $9 million in cash and more than $7 million in in-kind goods and services to school/business partnerships in Florida.

The Atlanta Partnership for Education

Atlanta, Georgia public schools have added two new partnership goals to the eight systemwide educational goals for *Atlanta 2000*, already in place. Partnership goals of the Atlanta Partnership for Education are the following:

1. Adults in Atlanta will be provided the opportunity to become literate, acquire the knowledge and skills necessary to compete in a global economy, and exercise the responsibilities of citizenship.
2. The Atlanta community will promote and support its public schools.

To achieve these goals, Atlanta Public Schools (APS) have established a five-step process for success. Vicki Gillespie, the Bank South representative (a planning partner in the Atlanta endeavor), indicated that

> The partnership planning process should be jointly undertaken by both the school and the business organization, preferably toward the end of one school year for the following school year. The plan should be developed so that the activities of the partnership reinforce the school's targeted objectives for the year. As many activities as reasonably possible should be evaluated for their effectiveness in assisting the school to attain its objectives. The plan should allow for a full notation of who is responsible for each activity and can be a working document as well as a complete display of the partner's intentions.

PROCESS STAGES

Step 1—*List school objectives* that the partnership will affect.

Step 2—*List activities/strategies.* Partners decide on specific activities to achieve the school's major goals for the year. This is achieved by a small working group from a mix of school, business, and community partnership representatives who determine what will be provided by the partner, including dates, frequency of contact, and people who will be active participants.

Step 3—*Establish benchmarks* to be used in evaluating the success of activities in meeting the objectives. Baseline data are linked to school goals (e.g., attendance figures, number of participants, test scores, etc.).

Step 4—*Determine result/evaluation.* Using the benchmarks in Step 3, evaluate measurable objectives and activities set forth in Steps 1 and 2. The evaluation should demonstrate that "the partnership activities are relative to the objectives and that they result in substantial progress for the school."

Step 5—*Record quantitative information* and report annually on the partnership activities, including the following information:

- The number of volunteers who participate
- The number of hours donated
- What in-kind and/or actual cash contributions were made

50 GREAT WAYS TO GIVE BACK TO YOUR BUSINESS PARTNER

The following are ideas from the Atlanta Public Schools:

1. Write thank-you notes.
2. Provide artwork for display at the business site.
3. Send cards (birthdays, holidays, etc.).
4. Send baked goods.
5. Make your athletic facilities, meeting rooms, and auditorium available to your partners at no cost.
6. Loan audiovisual and other equipment.
7. Provide seasonal decorations for lobby/reception area, employee lounge, or lunchroom.
8. Have homerooms or classes "adopt" employees.
9. Provide items for company bulletin board.
10. Provide displays (academic fair entries, projects, etc.) for lobby or lounge.
11. Design logo or other artwork for business partners.
12. Design note pads, signs, greeting cards, and so on for partners.
13. Assist with entertainment for special programs (chorus, band, dancers).
14. Invite partners to breakfast or lunch *on a regular basis.*
15. Do typesetting, layout, and printing for partners on items such as company newsletter, business cards, programs for special events, and so on.
16. Provide tickets to special community events.

17. Provide passes for school events (sports, drama, music, etc.).
18. Invite partners to school activities.
19. Keep partners informed of school activities.
20. Present partners with copy of school publications (yearbooks, literary magazines, brochures, and folders). Multiple copies are nice when practical.
21. Provide an old-fashioned pep rally for celebrations (production awards, safety awards, etc.).
22. Recognize a Partner of the Month or Year.
23. Recognize partners at Honors Day or Honors Night.
24. Host Partner's Night or Partner's Day at sporting events. Salute partners in the program. Hang banners in their honor. Have reserved seating for partners.
25. Host picnic with activities to allow partners to become better acquainted with students and staff.
26. Hold classes for company employees in vocational areas (woodworking, auto repair, powder-puff mechanics, horticulture).
27. Arrange for media coverage for activities between you and your partners.
28. Provide classes to help partners brush up on computer or typing skills.
29. Offer adult education or GED literacy for partners on site.
30. Provide foreign language classes.
31. Participate with partners in charitable events or choose a community project.
32. Create photo album of activities for partners.
33. Feature volunteers in media releases and internal newsletters. Send multiple copies to partners.
34. Provide car wash for partners.
35. Help clean up or landscape company grounds.
36. Provide copies of pictures taken during activities for use on company bulletin board.

37. Make placemats or tent-fold signs for use in company cafeteria.

38. Offer employee workshops on topics such as parenting skills, coping with stress, and how to help children with homework.

39. Host tours or open houses for company employees.

40. Build needed items for company (gazebo, shelves).

41. Provide part-time clerical help during busy times.

42. Provide videotaping assistance.

43. Have students make "Partners in Education" banner for the company.

44. Make and present pins, ribbons, or medals to partners.

45. Paint mural in the company lunchroom, lounge, or lobby.

46. Paint a picture of the company's building to hang in its lobby.

47. Have students develop safety posters for the company.

48. Develop a scrapbook of company activities.

49. Host annual sporting event between the school and business partners (volleyball, basketball, table tennis, etc.).

50. Ask your partners for suggestions on what your school could do for them. This is a great way to please your partners!

The Enterprise Ambassador Program

When Dave Thomas, the founder of Wendy's, first met Pam Masters, it was 1982, and she had a little home cooking restaurant in downtown Louisville, Kentucky. Five years later, after both Pam and Dave (and their respective families) had relocated to Florida, they became reacquainted through a mutual friend. Both Pam and Dave were concerned about kids, and it was not long before Pam started working for Mr. Thomas. (The title on her business card was RHP—initials for Right-Hand Person). The Enterprise Ambassador Program (EAP) was born in 1988. Founding members were Dave, Pam, and two representatives of the Chamber of Commerce. Dave had presented an award to a high school student with potential leadership skills, and he strongly voiced the need for youth to learn about the free enterprise system and understand the opportunities and responsibilities of America's unique economic system. Mr. Thomas would say, "Where else but in America could a 14-year-old busboy, like myself, have the opportunity to be able to develop a huge organization like Wendy's?"

Through Dave's philosophy and contacts, the program unfolded, and Pam became totally wrapped up in the day-to-day development and administration of the program. In 1990, Nova Southeastern University bought into EAP and Pam went with it. Dave Thomas is still encouraging growth and independence for youth and is active in EAP. He hopes that this program can be expanded into schools across the United States through the efforts of school/business partners.

EAP is based on Dave Thomas's personal entrepreneurship. Its director, Pam Masters, says that both teachers and students have responded warmly to the opportunities provided by this program.

The program introduces high school juniors to the concepts and practice of the business world they will enter as adults. Through a carefully orchestrated mix of classroom sessions, real-world experiences, and social consciousness-raising, these young people gain knowledge and insight that provide a firm foundation for future success.

High school juniors representing the 31 public, private, and alternative high schools in Broward County, Florida, are admitted to the program based on their interest in business, their desire to succeed, and their leadership potential. In the months that follow, they participate in four major program elements:

1. A 6-day summer institute at Nova Southeastern University, conducted by the American Management Association's Operation Enterprise, combines informative lectures with a competitive computer simulation of an actual business situation.
2. Nine monthly sessions with a personal mentor from the local business community provide a well-rounded glimpse of the "real world of business."
3. Monthly seminars enhance the students' personal development, interpersonal relationships, and business skills. Topics include business planning, effective public speaking, negotiation skills, and advice on college selection.

4. A community service project, designed and implemented by the students, benefits a local charity. Involvement does not end with completion of the program. During their senior year of high school, alumni make presentations to elementary students to share information and advice about what it takes to succeed in the free enterprise system. The message includes the importance of a plan, organization, self-discipline, and strong values, starting with development of good habits right now.

Benefits of EAP are felt by the students themselves, their mentors, and the community. Students gain a unique education in the world of business that gives them a competitive edge in college and their future careers. As one participant testified, "The Enterprise Ambassador Program has exposed me to the special people and talents that are the driving force of today's economy. It has given me the experience and initiative to go forward in the business world."

FUNDING THE PARTNERSHIP

EAP represents a dynamic partnership between education and the business community. Both public and private schools in Broward County make a financial contribution for each of their enrollees, and mentors match that amount. Additional monetary support is solicited from corporate and individual sponsors.

NEXT STEPS

Currently, EAP is in a restructuring mode, enabling it to adapt to the needs of many more students in the Broward County schools. For more information, contact Pam Masters, The Enterprise Ambassador Program, SBE Nova Southeastern University, 3301 S.W. 9th Ave., Ft. Lauderdale, FL 33315, (305) 424-5764.

Critical Questions to Ask for Maintaining Successful Partnerships

The quality of partnership activities may well determine a partnership's longevity. Ask yourself the following essential questions:

1. Are these components in place for your partnership program?
   - A clear organizational structure
   - Leadership and support staffs
   - A budget for your program
   - Management and record-keeping tools for program administration
2. Does your program have these components under development?
   - Set procedures for communication with partners
   - Selected activities designated for particular program purposes, based on both priority needs and fiscal resources
   - Procedures and record-keeping forms for program monitoring and evaluation

If you are developing a partnership program, ask and answer these key questions to guide the process. A stakeholder group might provide financial experts and/or helpful dollars to assist you in exploring possibilities.

Multiple Advantages of Partnerships

- Partnerships provide learning opportunities for students, staff, administrators, parents, and the business community, and linkage opportunities throughout the region, state, and nation.
- Partners enhance support for the educational environment by providing needed dollars for basic skills projects, enrichment programs, career education activities, and other programs facing severe budget cuts.
- Partnerships encourage the backing of critical political allies during budget time. Such support can counteract negativism and criticism of district spending.
- Partnerships provide good public relations for education through a perception within the community that its schools are effective. Offer shared services to the business community through extending effective and efficient preemployment training at lower cost or recruit entry-level employees who have good basic skills. Provide other human resources to meet individual needs of service users.

- Finally, partnerships help develop improved community relations and a positive image of your district with local corporations. Through employer participation, a business builds company morale and offers valuable leadership opportunities for employees.

What Business Partners Can Provide

Advisory members
Speakers
Field trips
Academic mentors/tutors
Employee loans
Student interns
Teacher interns
Printing
Equipment
Building improvement loans
Fundraising
Trophies, certificates, and other awards to students
Mentors
Cash

TIP: Make the funder a key stakeholder in your plan!

Summary

Given careful planning and skillful implementation, your school/business partnership can provide strong support for achieving educational goals within your community. Partnerships, like external funds from successful proposals, extend the impact of education through additional, competitive resources.

Chapter 3 will provide information to help you make important decisions about where and when to send your proposal. Sample proposals are presented as guidelines for proposal development. Budgets are discussed and analyzed in detail, and experienced grant proposal writers provide tips for the novice grantwriter.

3

Writing the Proposal

Chapter Highlights

- Your Case for Support
- Deciding Where and When to Send Your Proposal
- Writing the Grants Proposal
- What to Include in the Proposal
- Developing the Budget: Sample Budgets
- Generic Proposals: Pros and Cons
- Tips from Experts

Prior to writing any proposal, carefully analyze key issues to maximize your potential to realize funding. Most funding sources are interested in solving problems and in supporting positive changes.

Your Case for Support

Present your problem or concerns as representing a class of problems or as a specific example of a general concern of interest to the funder. As you develop your proposal, relate the purpose of your project to the goals of a specific program of the funding agency.

Supporting data for your problem will be part of the rationale that you are presenting to support your request for funds. Although you may have a detailed needs section later, in your rationale or introduction section, a modest data table might highlight key points by using census or other recognized data sources to demonstrate how your local or area problem is representative of the larger class of problems nationwide.

Either at the beginning or at the end of this introductory section, state the problem (or the specific purpose) of the project very concisely—in one or two sentences, at most. Highlight the brief statement by setting it out in text through underlining or a "bullet." (One example appears below.)

- The purpose of _____ is to develop, test, and evaluate the _____ as a process to remediate demonstrated high rates of student absenteeism in middle grades (i.e., Grades 7 through 9).

If you are not certain about a funder's goals, research and answer the following question before developing your proposal.

What is this funder looking for?

ANSWER: Funders generally seek projects that are ambitious, provide cost-effective use of financial resources, have long-lasting educational effects, address one sample of a common problem, and provide great public relations for the funder. An inquiry letter and a careful review of the funder's priorities and prior annual reports will help you get a good match between your ideas and the priorities of a funding source.

What Funders Are or Are Not Looking for

According to grantmakers, the three most common weaknesses in nonfunded proposals (Coley & Scheinberg, 1990) in 1989 were

1. The problems addressed were insignificant—44%.
2. How monies will be used is unclear—42%.
3. The nature of the problem is unclear—33%.

How can you avoid these weaknesses in developing your proposal?

Covering these topics in detail will help you convince the funder that your project is significant because *the primary reason that proposals remain unfunded is that the funder remains unconvinced of the "significance" of the project*—the grantmaker does not consider the project important enough to fund. The second reason for rejection of submitted proposals is lack of clarity with respect to proposed budgets. When identifying resources needed, your case should detail use of funds (as linked to priorities of funder). Third, the nature of the problem must be visible to the proposal reader. Your presentation of the problem should elicit a colorful picture of your setting. Discuss the proposal with others who may present arguments that you have not considered—this may help make your case more convincing.

Fundamentals of Your Case for Support

1. Provide a clear picture of your school site—demographics, curriculum, special programs, best features, and the problem.

2. Clearly present the needs you are attempting to meet, with supporting data about impact of needs on the quality of education provided to students.

3. Articulate the plan you are proposing to meet these needs, including how the plan was developed. Provide a comprehensive picture of reasons why this plan is the best means to address the educational needs. Support your ideas with other successful models and provide a timetable for implementation.

4. Outline direct and indirect educational benefits derived through successful implementation of your plan. Emphasize the impact of your project on the quality of education and its implication for the individual student.

5. List anticipated costs for your plan. Depending on what the funder is seeking, you may need to convince the funder that you have given careful attention to costs and that you can complete the project within your budget.

6. Provide an evaluation design for your plan as part of your implementation timeline. Tie it to measurable objectives.

7. Provide a convincing argument about the professional and personal qualifications of the proposed project director.

8. Delineate future funding needs and a strategy to secure needed resources.

9. Develop a plan to continue the project after initial funding is completed. How will you institutionalize the grant?

10. Provide appropriate support information in appendixes.

11. Develop a calendar with your agenda for grant follow-up. Specify important targeted grant deadlines and appointments on this calendar to ensure ongoing contact with the funder. Details of stewardship activities could be added here. Make it easy for the grant manager to take one glimpse at the calendar and see any glaring deadlines that may be anticipated.

Deciding Where and When to Send Your Proposal

Corporations and foundations that fund education projects tend to be regionally oriented, with some important exceptions (see Resource D at the end of the book). They frequently fund projects in schools within their business locales. In this way, companies may both help their employees and expand their visibility as benefactors in the area. A first step is to seek a funding source that has substantial business or service involvement in your geographic area. Public funding sources have programs with specific purposes.

Timing may be everything. Some funders accept unsolicited proposals from individuals and school districts four times a year; others accept proposals only two or three times yearly. Some funders accept proposals on a year-round basis. Responses to public source "Requests for Proposals," or RFPs, have specific deadline dates.

Factors Considered by Foundations in the Selection Process

A survey of foundations ranked the following as the top six factors affecting whether or not an education project gets funded (Ruskin, 1988). The project

- Has cost-effective organization
- Works in tandem with other agencies and groups
- Reflects cultural diversity and sensitivity
- Is administered by a person who has a proven track record
- Implements an imaginative and innovative program
- Receives funding from other sources

In its Contributions' Policy, the American Honda Foundation (AHF) lists what the foundation is seeking and states, "In reviewing grant-making opportunities, the following questions, among others, will be considered."

- Is the program national in intent, impact, and outreach?
- Is it broad in scope?
- Does the request fall within the scope of the AHF guidelines and grantmaking policies?
- Are the objectives and programs of the organization seeking funding clearly defined and reasonably capable of achievement?
- Does the program have merit?
- Are the organization's objectives and programs supportive of the public and the interests of American Honda Motor Co., Inc.?
- Does the proposed activity serve a needed function, without the creation of undesirable program duplication?
- Where will the program be and what is planned in the next 3 to 5 years?
- Have the organization and its leaders demonstrated, by past accomplishment, an ability to fulfill the stated objectives and successfully implement their programs?
- Is the organization both efficiently and ethically managed?
- What is the maturity and competency level of the administrators of the program or agency?
- Who is on the organization's board of directors?
- Does the organization have an active governing board and support from the community?
- What is the financial status of the organization and what are the sources of its income? Does it have a broad base of support?
- Does the program propose untried methods that ultimately may result in providing solutions to the complex cultural, educational, scientific, and social concerns currently facing the American society?
- What are the potential risks to funding this program? What are the adverse consequences and/or potential problems involved?
- What are the pros and cons to funding?

- How urgent is the funding priority of this program?
- Is the program dreamful, imaginative, innovative, creative, and humanistic?
- What is the potential impact of the program?

What Type of Grant Are You Seeking?

There are various types of grants, and the type of grant that you are seeking may help determine where you send your proposal. For example, some sources do not support research or capital projects, some sources support only nonprofit or public agencies, and so on. AHF awards these 10 types of grants to nonprofit organizations:

- Seed grants
- Operating grants
- Project/program grants
- General support/continuing support grants
- Challenge grants
- Matching grants
- Conditional grants
- Scholarship and fellowship grants
- Multiyear grants (up to 2 years)
- Proactive grants

TIP: Funding from multiple funding sources is highly thought of by funders. An individual funder does not want to have the entire fiscal responsibility for your project but wants to share this burden.

Writing the Grants Proposal

Introduction

Whether you are developing a proposal for private funding or for public support, provide your information in a logical manner that the reviewer can follow. As you are preparing your proposal (any of the parts, as well as the total proposal), organize your work so that the general flow of information proceeds from general to specific (Brewer, Achilles, & Fuhriman, 1995). Thus, when you develop the project

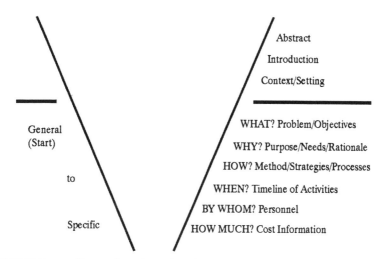

FIGURE 3.1. General-to-Specific Flow of Proposal Categories

needs, first discuss national needs, then regional needs, state and area needs, and finally, local needs.

The questions that guide news reporting can help structure the general-to-specific elements of a proposal. The What? and Why? questions provide a framework for moving from a general problem area (what the need is) to the highly specific aspect of putting a dollar figure or cost on particular aspects of your plan or procedures. The budget section is the most explicit and detailed because it must specify the value that is placed on each effort in terms of the dollars and time to be allocated to that effort. The budget answers the question How Much?

The What? and Why? questions are much more general than How Much? They tend to be philosophic or broad in nature and should lead into the proposal. Moving from general to specific lets the reader know the planning and the line of thought that you are following in the development of the project.

GENERAL  SPECIFIC

Figure 3.1, which represents a funnel in appearance, graphically represents the general-to-specific aspect of the total proposal. The situation explained above using needs as the example shows a specific application of the general-to-specific procedure in one section of a proposal. The proposal may also contain an abstract and a brief introduction (or context and setting information)

Major Sections of a Proposal

There are some major headings or sections that one would expect to find in a proposal. These broadly include (a) the problem statement or research question (What?), (b) the context or setting for the study (Why?), (c) a philosophic or literature base (Why? and How?), (d) the general methodology or procedures in the project (How?), (e) a statement of project duration and major events—timeline (When?), (f) project personnel (By Whom?), and (g) budget or fiscal information (How Much?). Specific agency or proposal guidelines may require more or less information or information in a different order from that provided here. The proposer must follow the specific agency guidelines. Consider the general information provided here as being only a generic example.

Before the body of the proposal itself, you may present an abstract or summary of project plans. Some project writers prepare this section last and develop it in easy-to-read "media" language—clear, concise, and cogent. Ask a good writer or a professional editor to critique your writing as you prepare this section so it is clear and jargon free.

You may need a brief introduction to the entire project, perhaps tying it to some national initiative that has helped focus project efforts. Make this connection early in your narrative, by showing the relationships in a diagram such as the one below.

National Initiative(s)	Funder's Purposes	Project's Objectives
1. America 2000 Goals	1.	1.
2. Dropout Prevention	2.	2.
3. Violence Reduction	3.	3.

TIP: There may be no need for a separate budget in the initial proposal or contact letter. Check funder guidelines.

CONTEXT AND SETTING

This section, usually quite brief, may consist of two parts. One part is basic information about your agency or group and its potential for being successful in conducting the proposed project. This information will acquaint the funder with key aspects of your agency: size, complexity, purposes and philosophy, prior interests and funding support, personnel resources, and your agency's track record or history of success. Emphasize that your agency has, or will obtain through this grant, all of the framework or structure to conduct the proposed activity. You might explain briefly the location of your agency and any pertinent travel or geographical support available (airports, major roads, bus routes).

A second type of context information relates to your knowledge of the current status of the problem you plan to address and your understanding of other work in the same or similar conceptual areas. This second arena, sometimes called a research and literature review, is important in research and development (R&D) projects or in projects dealing with social issues and change. In this section, you will show how your activity (project, research problem) fits into any ongoing effort and how it addresses key policy issues or problems.

THE WHAT? THE PROBLEM
STATEMENT OR OBJECTIVES

The problem statement explains clearly and concisely the problem, the research question, or the objectives of your project idea. Below are some sample problem statements, objectives, and research questions.

Sample Problem Statements

- Minority students are 20% of the student body at X school, but they constitute 35% of the out-of-school suspensions (OSS). We desire a more representative distribution of OSS while reducing the total suspensions.
- Females are 51% of the junior and senior classes at Y school, but they account for only 10% of the enrollments in advanced math and science classes. This underrepresentation wastes human potential and perpetuates unsound stereotypes.

Sample Research Questions

- What is the impact of schoolwide training in and subsequent use of (a) peer mediation and (b) other conflict-resolution strategies on student behavior as related to out-of-school suspension?
- Does intensive career and academic counseling for females in math and science processes and careers at Grades 9 and 10 serve to increase the percentage of females in advanced math and science courses in Grades 11 and 12 in subsequent years?

Sample Objectives

The following project objectives are based on the extensive needs data collected at the ABC School. Supporting data tables appear in the next section.

Project activities of the ABC School "Neighborhood/School Project" are designed to achieve the following objectives:

1. To select and train at least 15 peer mediators from among the members of each grade (Grades 9-12) of the ABC School.
2. To select and train a cadre of at least 10 ABC School faculty to direct, advise, and monitor the Neighborhood/School Project.
3. To reduce the total out-of-school suspension (OSS) rates at ABC School from _____% to _____% by 19XX through a program of student behavior training in conflict resolution strategies such as _____, _____, and _____.
4. To reduce the disproportionate representation of minority students in OSS by a program of school, parent, and agency collaboration that . . .

THE WHY? NEEDS, PURPOSES, AND RATIONALE

You may include both a problem statement and several objectives to show a connection between your objectives and the problem. These will build upon a clear presentation of the needs that precipitated your project. The needs data are important because they serve as a baseline or benchmark against which to measure project success. After all, the ultimate in project success is to remove the problem or to reduce the need for that project. Clear definitions of problems are easier if you have compiled accurate and cogent needs data. Follow the general-to-specific framework in your needs process, showing the needs trend from world or national to regional or state to local, getting more and more detailed as you present the needs relating to your specific project.

Sample Needs Narrative

The national trend toward youth violence is reflected in major news headlines: "Teen Gangs Terrorize Halls of X School" (*USA Now*, 6/6/XX, p. 1); "National Study Shows 1 in 5 Youths Carry Weapons to School" (*NY Tribune*, X/X/XX, p. A-1); "Metro Gang Recruiters Target ABC School OSS Students" (*Hometown Weekly Clarion*, X/X/XX, p. 1); "The X State Commission on Violence in Schools Reported _____ and Recommended That School Faculties _____" (Commission Report, X/X/XX, p. 1). [This will be supported by data tables as appropriate.]

The ABC School has witnessed escalating youth violence similar to that reported nationwide. For example, in 1980 the overall percentage of total suspensions (not just pupils suspended) for fighting, assault, and weapons was 12%; by 19XX it had increased to 49% (i.e., nearly one half of all suspensions were for violent offenses). In 1980 only 4 students in a student body of 1,206 had been adjudicated and sent to youth detention for weapons violations; in 19XX the comparable figures were 93 of 1,265. Table A shows the trends in annual referrals of students for weapons violations at four levels.

TABLE A Annual Referrals of Students for Weapons Violations, Showing the Increasing Rate at School XYZ Compared to Benchmarks

Site	Years					Difference
	1991	1992	1993	1994	1995	1991-1995
National	3.9	4.0	4.0	4.0	4.0	+ .1
State X	4.1	4.1	4.2	4.2	4.2	+ .1
ABC District	4.6	4.7	4.7	4.8	4.8	+ .2
XYZ School	4.6	4.7	4.9	4.9	5.2	+ .6

The weapons referral rate at Grade 9, traditionally high in U.S. schools, has been increasing slowly since 1991. The national trend is reflected in State X, which has a referral rate slightly greater than the United States (and ranks 38 out of 50 nationally). The ABC District's rate is considerably worse than the state average, ranking 47 out of 51 districts. The Grade 9 weapons referral rate in XYZ School, although at the state average in 1991, has continued to grow worse than the state average, ranking currently (1995) among the worst in a state that is near the bottom among all states in the United States. Table A shows these comparisons, including the dramatic change for the worse (1991-1995) at XYZ School.

Not only must we reduce school violence, but suspension as a punishment for violence seems to lead to youth membership in gangs in nearby Gotham City (see *Hometown Clarion*, X/XX/XX, p. 1). Data from this survey reveal that (a) _____, (b) _____, (c) _____, and (d) _____ . Thus, the project as described here will fulfill an important need and will become a model for other small and midsize communities bordering big cities.

A recent (X/XX/XX) survey was distributed to all students at XYZ School and sent to a 20% random sample of student households (62% return). The returned surveys showed the following:

Item	Students (98%) Yes No N/A	Parents (62%) Yes No N/A	Totals Yes No N/A
1. _____ .			
2. _____ .			
3. _____ .			

THE HOW? METHODS, STRATEGIES, ACTIVITIES, AND EVALUATION PLANS

Sample Statement of Method

The major solution strategies and activities of this project are 1). . . . ., 2). . . . ., 3). . . . ., 4). . . . ., 5). . . . . To measure the success of (1 through 5 above), evidence of each major activity will be collected through the following data collection processes:

1. Ongoing direct observations of specific student behaviors within the classroom
2. One-on-one interviews with targeted students
3. Focus group interviews with parents, teachers, community agencies, and so on

Sample Timeline of Major Activities

Activity(ies)	Date(s)	Narrative
1. Classroom observation		
a. Pretest	10/1/XX-12/15/XX	At least 10 hours per week in Grade 9 English classes at both pre and post
b. Posttest	5/1/XY-6/15/XY	
2. Interviews (Focus groups)	(Week of. . .)	
a. Students		
Pre_____	12/5 and 12/12/XY	Presessions will
Post_____	6/1 and 6/8/XY	obtain data for training and for process adjustment
b. Parents		
Pre_____	1/20 and 1/27/XY	Postsessions will
Post_____	6/1 and 6/8/XY	obtain feedback on procedures and successes or failures
c. Agency representative		
Pre_____	11/7 and 11/14/XX	
Post_____	5/15 and 5/22/XY	
3. Intervention steps		
a. Information dissemination Parent meetings Agency reps Student "rap" session	10/XX-3/XY and 5/XY-6/XY	Provide school-agency and community information on project and support systems

Activity(ies)	Date(s)	Narrative
b. Training		18-24 student
Peer mediation	11/15-12/15/XX	mediators and 4-6 faculty mentors
Parent support	10/5-11/4/XX	Neighborhood "safe havens"
Other conflict resolution	11/4-12/1/XX	2-3 violence alternatives
c. Implementation Violence-reduction processes	1/1-6/20/XY	20-24 monitors

THE HOW MUCH? BUDGET, FISCAL INFORMATION, AND COSTS DETAIL

Your budget is your estimated plan for use of funds. During a project, you may need to make one or more changes in your original estimate by following the funding agency's rules for budget modifications, but your original budget will explain major project costs and allocate them to categories such as personnel, fringe benefits, supplies and materials, travel, consultant help, equipment, and so on.

Your initial contact with a funding source (a letter of inquiry or a brief prospectus) may require only a very general budget, perhaps just a single estimate of total funds needed. This "ballpark estimate" provides planning information so that funding agency personnel can place your request into a category, such as a small grant needing only limited review and action by a program officer or a large grant needing detailed review and full board action. At a later time, however, you will need to provide a detailed budget as part of your comprehensive proposal.

Provide specific financial information requested by the funder. Collect financial information, if necessary, before beginning the application-writing process. Grant guidelines or application forms will explain the exact and specific information you need. Supply adequate fiscal data to make your case, and present it clearly and concisely. Do not omit requested data, even if immediately unavailable. Obtain the assistance of teachers, board members, comptrollers, CPAs, legal experts, and so on to ensure compliance with the funding agency's requests for information. Designate a special committee to read, react to, and edit the budget to ensure that you have covered all required items and developed an accurate estimate of funds needed to conduct your project.

At the conclusion of your project, you will be required to provide a carefully documented and accurate accounting of the exact expenditures by budget categories. A budget is an estimate of expenditures to be made by categories, whereas your financial report represents a detailed statement of actual expenditures.

Fiscal Information About Your Agency

Some funding sources will request information about your agency's fiscal condition, such as the current or prior year's budget and source(s) of funds. Typically, this information is not requested or required in detail until your project has received at least an initial positive review by the funding source and you are preparing a final proposal. It may not be required for small grants or for awards from some agencies (such as from a state agency if your agency is also a governmental agency).

This fiscal information should be available from your business office, treasurer, or comptroller, or in year-end financial reports and in current operating budgets of your organization. You may need to rearrange some of your organization's reporting categories to meet the funding agency's requests for categorical information, but you should provide all of the essential data.

Sample of Fiscal Information Requested by a Foundation

A sophisticated proposal writer provides all information sought by the funding source. Several questions on the American Honda Foundation's (AHF) application form require fiscal information about the applicant. The funder requires that an applicant demonstrate fiscal knowledge about the nonprofit organization and its programs, so the proposal writer should demonstrate a thorough understanding of the funding of his or her organization. Knowledge of how short-term activities (e.g., your project) relate to long-range organizational planning, especially as related to budgetary issues, should be reflected in the application.

Building a Budget Document

If possible, keep your budget simple while still providing the detail that will allow reviewers to judge your project. Allocate requested funds to categories so that your project activities and budget support each other. Each project activity should show justification for each expenditure and its importance to project success. For example, do not try to sneak added equipment, such as computers, into the budget. If your project is to provide instruction to a group, develop personnel costs to show the *instruction* emphasis. That might require explicit personnel budget definition as shown here in capital letters.

> I. Personnel
>   A. Administration
>   B. INSTRUCTION
>   C. Support (clerical, etc.)

A *narrative budget* that explains the basis for each cost right next to the cost is a convenient and effective way to display your costs and the way that you arrived at them. Alternatively, you might use just a summary budget and then explain on a separate budget narrative page the way that you arrived at each cost displayed on the summary budget. Some proposals may require a detailed budget in the budget section and a summary budget on the required proposal forms (boilerplate).

Major budget categories are listed below. Each category is explained and demonstrated in the succeeding sections.

> I.   Personnel costs (including fringe benefits)
> II. Nonpersonnel costs
> III. Indirect costs (where these are allowed)
> IV. Total costs

Unless you are instructed to the contrary, two types of funds are reported in the budget. They are the funds that you are requesting from the funding agency and matching, donated, or in-kind support for your project.

Personnel costs include planned expenditures for each person who will be on the staff for your project. Some agencies ask that you include here consultant costs, honoraria, and extra pay such as hourly rates for persons who may be participants in your activities. Most agencies, however, ask that you include here *only* the salary and fringe benefits for your staff personnel and include consultants (etc.) in a separate category under "nonpersonnel costs." In examples used here, only your staff costs are shown as "personnel"; consultants are shown as "nonpersonnel" items.

- Show the personnel cost basis for each item, including the percentage of time devoted to the project by all (e.g., 100%, 20 days/yr., .33 time, etc.).
- Estimate fringe benefits as a percentage of salaries and wages, or list each fringe separately, such as FICA, health, life insurance, or unemployment. The percentage method (e.g., fringe benefits computed at 25% of salaries and wages, or S&W) is easier and allows a cleaner budget document. *Check this estimate with your budget expert to be sure that it is correct.* Examples for personnel and fringe benefits shown here are provided as a narrative, 12-month budget.

	Total
I. Personnel (12 months)	
A. Administration	
Director J. Smith, 100%, $50,000/yr	$50,000
Adm. Asst. J. Doe, 37.5%, $40,000/yr	15,000
B. Instruction	
3 teachers, 100%, $40,000/yr	120,000
2 teacher assts., 100%, $25,000/yr	50,000
C. Support staff/secretarial	
1 clerk typist, 100%, $25,000	25,000
SUBTOTAL (S&W)	260,000
D. Fringe benefits: Insurance, etc. (25% S&W)	65,000
TOTAL Personnel	$325,000

The next example uses an 18-month budget estimate for personnel and shows costs distributed into (a) requests from the funding agency (grantee) and (b) in-kind or matching contributions of the recipient agency. Totals of both sources are also provided in this narrative budget example.

	Grantee	In-Kind	Total
I. Personnel (18 months)			
A. Administration			
Director .50 @ $6,000/mo.	$ 54,000	0	$54,000
Adm. asst. 2/3 @ $3,000/mo.	18,000	18,000	36,000
B. Instruction			
Teacher @ $3,000/mo.	54,000	0	54,000
Teacher asst. 1/3 @ $1,800/mo.	0	10,800	10,800
C. Support staff .50 @ $2,000/mo.	18,000	0	18,000
SUBTOTAL (S&W)	144,000	28,800	172,800
D. Fringe benefits (@ .25)	36,000	7,200	43,200
TOTAL	$180,000	$36,000	$216,000

Nonpersonnel costs include planned expenditures for project operations, exclusive of (a) personnel (staff salaries and wages) and (b) indirect costs (if they are allowed). The next example disregards indirect costs and shows as a part of the direct cost most items that might be in a negotiated indirect cost (or overhead) rate.

The overhead or *indirect cost* computation (if allowed) lets you avoid the task of computing detailed direct costs for such things as utilities, janitorial service, and other "shared" costs. (One author suggests that you do not now need to estimate and cost out the rolls of toilet paper required for the project duration.)

Direct cost categories include such things as per diem and travel, supplies and materials, equipment directly related to the project, consultant costs (honoraria and travel), communications (phone, fax, mail), space or rental, utilities, and other. (Use "other" sparingly. It might include hourly rates for participants, allowable food or meeting costs, utilities, custodial, etc.)

Process to Generate "Matching" Funds

Note the strategies used to develop and show local effort as matching or in-kind contribution. Some agencies require matching funds; but even if matching support is not required, the delineation of such support sends to the funding agency a message about the importance of the project and your attention to cost efficiency.

	Grantee	In-Kind	Total
II. Nonpersonnel costs			
A. Travel			
1. Airfare for 3 meetings, est. 2 project personnel @ \$500/trip/person ($500 \times 3 \times 2$)	3,000	0	3,000
2. Per diem @ \$50 or less (actual costs), est. 20 days, 20×50	1,000	0	1,000
3. Lodging (actual rate, est. @ \$90 $\times$ 20 nights)	1,800	0	1,800
4. Local auto mileage @ 20,000 mi. @ \$.30 (\$.05 donated)	5,000	1,000	6,000
5. Parking fees/limo/taxi, est. \$100/trip	600	0	600
SUBTOTAL (Travel)	11,400	1,000	12,400
B. Supplies and materials			
1. General office supplies, est. @ \$300/mo. $\times$ 18 mo. for operations	3,600	1,800	5,400
2. Essentials: envelopes, folders, tape, staples, etc.	1,000	1,000	2,000
SUBTOTAL (S&M)	4,600	2,800	7,400
C. Equipment			
1. Essential office start-up			
Files (2) @ \$120 (4 drawer)	240		240
Desks (2) @ \$280 ea.	560		560
Desk chairs (2) @ \$190 ea.	380		380
Credenza, table	120		120
Word processor, hardware, software	1,800		1,800
SUBTOTAL (Equip.)	3,100		3,100

	Grantee	In-Kind	Total
D. Consultant costs			
1. Trainers in strategic planning* (25 participants) 2 @ $1,000/day × 4 days	8,000		8,000
Travel 2 air @ $600 ea.	1,200		1,200
Per diem 8 days @ $150 (food & lodging)	1,200		1,200
*Participants will become local facilitators to start school-community planning efforts.			
2. Local "follow-up" facilitators from schools			
8 days @ $200 ($200/day donated)	1,600	1,600	3,200
Local travel (auto) 8,000 × $.25 ($.05 donated)	2,000	400	2,400
3. Training supplies @ $40/ participant for community strategic planning facilitators	1,000	___	1,000
SUBTOTAL (Consult.)	15,000	2,000	17,000
E. Communication			
1. Phone, est. $80/mo. (local)		1,440	1,440
Long dist., est. $200/mo.	3,600		3,600
2. Fax, est. $100/mo. × 18 mo.		1,800	1,800
3. Postage rates, est. $200/mo. × 18 mo.	3,600	___	3,600
SUBTOTAL (Comm.)	7,200	3,240	10,440
F. Utilities and operating			
1. Pro rata costs for office, est. $400/mo. × 18 mo. (50/50 split)	3,600	3,600	7,200
2. Custodial	5,400		5,400
3. Supplies (cleaning)	3,600	___	3,600
SUBTOTAL (Oper.)	12,600	3,600	16,200

	Grantee	In-Kind	Total
G. Other			
1. Payment to participants for time, etc., est. $10/hr. × 100 people × 20 hrs.	20,000	10,000[a]	30,000
2. Refreshments at meetings	2,000	1,000[b]	3,000
3. Rental for meeting as needed, est.	1,200	1,200[b]	2,400
SUBTOTAL (Other)	$23,200	$12,200	$35,400

a. This rate is to reimburse the participants for their time. No expenses will be paid directly, such as travel. Travel to meetings is individual in-kind. These participants will form the nucleus of community teams; $5/hr. is estimated as in-kind.
b. Our agency will provide some coffee and soft drinks and supply meeting space for small groups.

Indirect Costs or Overhead

Some agencies have a negotiated indirect cost rate that they can use if the funding agency allows these charges (check with your fiscal officer). Basically, indirect costs or overhead rates are to pay for the operational, day-to-day items that are true costs but that are difficult to allocate to specific categories or to several concurrent activities. The overhead or indirect cost rate (for example, 10%) is computed on some predetermined base such as the total direct costs, or TDC, of the project. If and when you use an overhead rate, do not include in direct costs those categories that are part of the overhead, or the regular and usual cost of doing business (example: custodial, utilities, accounting, light bulbs, incidentals). For federal grants, these are specified in rules and regulations or in federal management circulars (FMCs). Using indirect costs makes your budget document easier to develop, less complicated, and cleaner in appearance. Your agency gets the indirect costs as its payment for housing and operating your project *after* you charge off to the project the legitimate *direct* costs.

The following is a sample budget developed using overhead or indirect cost rates. Essentially, it uses the same structure as the prior example, but not the same figures.

18-Month Budget Estimates	Grantee	In-Kind	Total
I. Personnel & fringe	$180,000	$36,000	$216,000
II. Nonpersonnel			
A. Travel	11,400	1,000	12,400
B. Supplies	4,600	2,800	7,400
C. Equipment	3,100		3,100
D. Consultant	15,000	2,000	17,000
E. Communication	7,200	1,800	9,000
F. Utilities[a]	N/A (indirect costs)		
G. Other	23,000	12,200	35,400
TOTAL DIRECT COSTS (TDC)	$244,300	$55,800	$300,300
Indirect costs (10% TDC)	$24,430	$5,580	$30,030
TOTAL COSTS	$268,730	$61,380	$330,330

a. Items are now part of indirect costs. Totals of categories E and F in the other computation were $10,440 and $16,200, respectively. The indirect rate of 10% provided a total of $30,030 compared to a total "direct method" of $26,640.

In this example, the indirect costs, or overhead, are computed on both the funds requested and the matching or in-kind support. This serves to increase slightly the matching of your agency. Some of the operational elements are removed (e.g., the $1,440 for local in-kind for the phone in the "communication" category, because this is now part of the overhead). The entire category called "utilities" is now removed.

If you do not spend the entire amount of your budget based on which indirect costs are computed, you will return to the grantee the pro rata share of indirect costs, too. If you overspend a little, your agency might contribute some of the indirect costs to help you out of the overexpenditure problem—but that local decision is clearly not a reason for any fiscal irresponsibility.

The budget section is the most specific part of the general-to-specific structure of your proposal. It shows the value or dollar cost of what you will do. If required to do so, you could divide your budget into categories, such as project phases, cost per month, instruction, administration, and so on. A detailed and accurate budget is a valued asset for your project, both for planning and for sharing cost efficiency.

TIP: Know and respect all deadlines! (There is no such thing as a late proposal.) Plan to have the proposal done at least 1 week before the deadline date to accommodate unexpected delays such as signatures, duplication, late assignments, and so on.

If proposal guidelines call for inclusion of a budget, provide a carefully delineated request. Indicate that you have carefully reviewed basic expenditures and have obtained accurate information.

TIP: Yours may be the greatest proposal submitted, but someone else has to be convinced your idea has merit.

An important component of a budget is the budget summary. The budget summary, although written after the budget is done, is presented at the beginning of the budget. A shortened sample format for a budget summary follows.

	Requested	Donated (In-Kind)	Total This Grant
A. Personnel			
1. Salaries			
2. Fringe benefits			
3. Contract services			
B. Nonpersonnel			
1. Operating costs			
2. Communication costs			
3. Travel costs			
4. Equipment costs			
5. Other costs			
C. Indirect costs			
D. Total			

Discussion of Budget Narrative

Note that costs in a "requested" column are items you are asking the funder to pay for. The next column ("matching" or "in-kind") is the "donated" column, which includes items supported from other funding sources, or goods or services in-kind. In the case of federal grants, these two columns represent the "federal share" and the "nonfederal share."

Staff salaries should not be combined with fringe benefits. If you are delineating grant benefits in detail, enter donated fringe benefits as payroll percentages.

For salaries and wages of staff, show only salaries that will be paid either from the grant you are proposing, from another funding source, or from your regular budget. Consultants, unpaid volunteers, and so on should be placed in a separate category.

Three categories of dollar amounts are appropriate for each budget type: total dollars, total dollars requested, and total donated dollars. Dollar totals requested from the funder, added to the totals of dollars already donated for the project, should add up to total dollars.

TIP: Try to limit the budget proposal to one page if included in the initial application.

More About Budgets

Anticipate that the grants manager has probably reviewed other, similar proposals and has a grasp of the "bottom-line" expenditures you will encounter in the process. Gather as much information as possible to estimate costs. The time you have taken to complete the budget will be reflected in the quality of the content. Clearly, budgets submitted along with initial proposal requests are only estimates in any case, but check budget details so that your presentations are *reasonable.* You are asking the funder to entrust you with substantial monies over some period of time to complete the project, so present sound data! Check and recheck budget details. Ask for enough, but don't be greedy. Depending on the flexibility of the specific funder, modest additional funding for your project may or may not be available while you are in the grant implementation phase.

This procedure can be replicated for other grant categories: non-personnel, rentals (project related), consumable supplies, travel, telephone, and other costs. Provide just the right amount of detail in the proposed budget. Make your point on needed dollars and provide only the supporting material requested by the grantmaker.

Even if you follow all the best advice from the experts, you may still have to be more innovative in finding a way to demonstrate the uniqueness of your proposal to a funder. Here is a "laundry list" of ideas to consider, garnered from a variety of sources.

1. An introductory videotape
2. Documentation of the problem setting beyond what is called for in grant guidelines; use of print media, statistics, and so on to support your case
3. Interviews with potential grant recipients
4. Clippings from national organizations, news reports on the condition of the grant recipient group expected to benefit from your proposal, and so on
5. Development of a formal coalition of groups that would benefit from the grant
6. A letter of support from the newly formed coalition with member names and positions on letterhead stationery
7. Use of emotional appeals by demonstrating students' needs through creative audiovisuals (e.g., a short video, a film, a book, or several books self-published by at-risk students)

The news media can be enlisted to support your program and provide input into your proposal. Local newspaper clippings that effectively present your case may be attached to a cover letter.

Before including any extra material to support your application, be sure to read the application guidelines carefully. Some grantors strictly enforce their page limits, and an application containing additional letters of support or media articles may cause the entire proposal to exceed the page limit, thus disqualifying it.

Grant Checklist

The following checklist will help you at the outset of the grant process.

_____ 1. Decide on your goals. Be clear about what you want to accomplish. Draw up both short-term and long-range plans (going ahead to 5 years into the project).

_____ 2. Review successful applications from other grantseekers from one or more of the foundations to which you are applying. Be sure that you have a good match between the funder's mission and project goals.

_____ 3. Spend some time in the library or on-line researching available funding. Jot down essential phone numbers and contact funders if you have questions. Be certain you have the correct name of the appropriate contact person.

_____ 4. Organize your time into areas of proposal writing, marketing, and grant management, with activities, budgets, and staff devoted to each segment. Develop a timeline for each activity.

_____ 5. Send a letter of intent prior to submitting the proposal, if possible. Check with the funder about this issue.

_____ 6. Devote an appropriate amount of time to each activity as per your particular needs. (A discussion of this issue follows.)

_____ 7. Carefully review all specific funder guidelines.

_____ 8. Keep the proposal as short as possible. Limit the number of pages to enhance its appeal to the reviewer.

_____ 9. Budget guidelines: Clearly delineate all major expenditures required for your project in the budget you present. You may not want to make it too detailed; for example, you may exclude small expenditures that add to costs such as stamps or stationery. Provide enough detail to cover the information requested by the funder.

_____ 10. Don't ask for more than you need.

_____ 11. Focus on your management skills in the proposal, augmenting them with your resumé and recommendations from important individuals or groups. Consider attaching information about honors you've received for professional or community work, special training received, and other positions held that illustrate your outstanding ability to direct your project.

_____ 12. Don't forget that marketing should be taken into account in these areas: the project design, the budget, your proposed project timeline, and your plan to evaluate the project.

_____ 13. Present a written plan to update the funder on a regular basis.

_____ 14. Present information about current research, literature, or projects that are linked to your proposal. Identify experts who will support your efforts.

_____ 15. Use your evaluation plan as a marketing tool.

_____ 16. Set up a meeting (if possible) or telephone conference (if no meeting can be arranged) to meet the funder personally before submitting the proposal.

TIP: *Be sure to thank all persons or groups that helped you; send copies to them of the final proposal (without all of the extra attachments).*

After you have received the grant, implement ongoing communication with your funder. It is vitally important that you arrange to talk with your funder throughout the project. Once you have won the award, check the reporting instructions that accompany your grant. Contact the grants manager if you have any questions about grant-reporting requirements or other accompanying stipulations.

Writing a Generic Proposal: Pros and Cons

You have fully worked out many of your project's aspects before sending it to the funder. This is a big time-saver! However, keep in mind that each foundation has its own unique characteristics, and funders do differ enormously from one to the other. For example, many funders may well be impressed if you show them you have received monies from other foundations for your project (important in cases where large sums are in question). Other foundations, however, do not consider such a request appropriate for their missions. These foundations will not fund your request if you have received matching dollars or other contributions. Check on and tailor your proposal to the foundation proposal guidelines. Each grantmaker presents a list of nonqualifying individuals and groups for its grants, usually set forth under "limitations" in application guidelines and published in most grant sources.

Developing a Generic Proposal for Funding

There are both advantages and disadvantages to developing a generic proposal for funding, that is, developing your concept in most of its aspects *before* you have identified a prospective funder. This is the procedure followed by many nonprofit applicants for foundation dollars. The primary reason is that it takes considerable time to search for the right funder for a project. After you have identified possible funders, you can modify the idea to meet the specific funder's particular mission.

TIP: Several people may help on the actual writing so that you can benefit from their composite of skills: budget, figures, planning, and so on. However, one person should be responsible for final production and for editing (so it does not look like a committee job).

Your Role as Project Director

Whether or not you have established personal contact with the funder—the "name-recognition stage"—you will want to assure the funder that you are in a position of authority and that the role you will have as project director is within your "sphere of influence." Here are a few ideas.

1. Obtain letters of support from your coworkers.
2. Present students' products that may reflect coincidentally their high regard for your teaching ability.
3. Provide evidence in your proposal of strong support by parents and parent groups.
4. Toot your own horn. Let the funder know about honors you have won or organizational leadership roles you have held.

5. If your project involves the community in a partnership project, let the funder know about your activities within the community that assist the population you are trying to help.
6. Let the funder know you are a hard worker—that any project you start not only is completed but is completed with a high degree of efficiency as well as creativity. This is especially important if you are requesting funding for a long-term project or if you plan to request grant renewal for a second year.
7. Be specific about the dollar amounts you are requesting.
8. Develop a collaborative effort with a higher education institution in your area to obtain funding for a joint education project from a private foundation.

TIP: When you send your proposal to the funding source, include one extra copy that is loose (fastened only with a paper clip) so that it can be used as a master copy for duplicating purposes.

Summary

Chapter 3 provided information about what funders are seeking, types of grants, writing the major sections of a grant proposal, and budget development. Major budget categories were summarized, and samples of narrative budgets and budgets listing nonpersonnel categories were explained. As you gain expertise in the grant proposal writing process, you will begin to seriously consider some of the arguments (both pro and con) regarding generic proposals that were presented in this chapter.

Chapter 4 provides in-depth interviews with major funders of education projects. Criteria used in scoring proposals are carefully delineated, as are samples of proposals that received large grant awards. These provide helpful guidelines for the proposal development process.

4

"Insider" Information

Chapter Highlights

- Interviews With Grant Managers
- Selection Criteria Used by Funders
- Funded and Nonfunded Proposals: Models for Analysis
- Strengthening Grant Partnerships
- Monitoring Grant Activities

Interviews With Funders: General Points

Grants administrators with primary responsibility for the ultimate selection of proposals for funding bring personal perspectives to the competitive review process. There is a wide range of possible structures for selection of grants proposals from one funder to another. One grants manager may have sole responsibility for selection at Foundation X, whereas Foundation Y may employ a proposal selection committee. The proposal writer may benefit from knowing about the selection process used by funders.

Interviews with people who award grants provide insights into what the funders are seeking. The interviews here provide useful information about both the funding process and the development of winning proposals.

Interviews With Grant Managers: The Funder's View

Kathryn Carey is the Manager of Grants for the American Honda Foundation (AHF). She has management responsibility for all fiscal administration of the foundation. Ms. Carey is responsible for the initial review of grant solicitations for conformance with established policy and also for proactive grantmaking. She analyzes and evaluates grant proposals, assesses potential funding risks, and provides the board of directors with funding recommendations. Additionally, she conducts site evaluations, researches and evaluates all grant solicitations, conducts postgrant monitoring and evaluations to protect foundation investments, ensures compliance with grant agreements, and provides technical assistance to grantseekers. She conducts training seminars in grantmaking for her peers and in grantseeking for clients. She annually directs $1.2 million in venture capital grants and an investment portfolio of $14 million in endowment funds.

The Grantmaking Process: Scoring Proposals

Ms. Carey provided insights into the grant selection process for grantseekers and cites these common errors in proposals:

1. Not asking for a specific sum
2. Not including a budget
3. Not including the required 3- to 5-year plan

She reveals the following regarding the processes used to screen the proposals:

Three people read, evaluate, and score every proposal submitted to the AHF. For *each proposal*, three weighted scores are added and divided by three to come up with an average or mean score. The mean scores are then recorded and the top 10% go on in the evaluation process to be eligible for a site visit.

The AHF proposal rating criteria are in Table 4.1.

TABLE 4.1 AHF Proposal Rating Schedule: Guidelines for Giving

Descriptor	Weight
Scientific	10
Youthful	10
Broad in scope	9
Financially sound	8
Soundly managed	8
Foresightful, forward thinking	7
Potential for success	7
Degree of duplicity	6
Dreamful, imaginative	5
Creative	4
Humanistic	3
Urgency	2
Risk	1
TOTAL: 13 categories	80 possible points

HITACHI GENERAL GRANT REVIEW CRITERIA

Dr. Del Roy is President of the Hitachi Foundation which supports projects that help all Americans address the multicultural, community, and global issues facing them. He provided the following grantmaking objectives and review criteria for proposals to Hitachi.

- Our aim is to help people and institutions adjust to changed global and societal circumstances and to develop the capacity to identify and solve problems.
- We fund projects in three categories—community development, education, and global citizenship.
- As a small Foundation with very limited resources, we cannot support anywhere near all the requests we receive. Nor can we provide continued support (beyond 5 years) to our grantees. Therefore, we need to be highly selective and strategic in our approach to grantmaking.

The foundation selects projects based on the following general criteria:

- Promotes collaboration across sectors, institutions, organizations, and individuals
- Reflects multidisciplinary approaches
- Values diversity of thought, action, and person
- Recognizes that individuals, schools, and organizations do not operate in isolation from one another—that real solutions to long-term problems are to be found in a systems approach
- Demonstrates an understanding of the demographic shifts affecting this country and the impact of global factors on local communities
- Has the potential for adaptation to other communities or for increasing the knowledge base in the field
- Actively involves the people being served by the project
- Provides an opportunity to link the foundation's work in community development, education, and corporate citizenship
- Leverages the foundation's funds to have far-reaching impact
- Offers the foundation an opportunity to provide leadership around critical issues

HITACHI SPECIFIC GRANT REVIEW CRITERIA

In addition to these general guidelines, the foundation has specific criteria for each of its program areas.

Community Development Criteria
- Develops and engages community leadership
- Brings a variety of community "actors" into contact with one another
- Helps build strong and accountable community institutions
- Explores innovative strategies to build community capacity to solve problems
- Makes effective use of resources while developing new resources for the community

Education Criteria
- Helps prepare people to be productive members of society
- Recognizes that schools can play an important role in building and stabilizing communities
- Develops the connections between schools, parents, and communities

- Uses a variety of instructional approaches
- Uses the arts or museums to increase opportunities for creativity and problem solving
- Links education and economic opportunity
- Uses community resources such as arts organizations, corporations, religious institutions, and community service organizations

HITACHI GRANT REVIEW PROCESS

1. Prescreen all incoming proposals. All proposals that do not conform with our guidelines are removed from the process at this time. At this time, the foundation also eliminates proposals that are not as competitive as others relative to the general criteria.

2. First review. Foundation staff review the remaining proposals based on the general and specific criteria, and they pose questions that need to be answered. Staff meet to discuss the proposals and select a smaller group for further consideration.

3. Second review. Foundation staff conduct a second review of these proposals. They note strengths, weaknesses, and specific questions. Staff meet to discuss the proposals and select a much smaller group (10-12 proposals) for further consideration.

4. Full proposals. Letters are sent to each of these applicants, requesting submission of a more detailed proposal. They are provided with guidelines for that proposal and are asked to call a foundation staff member regarding specific questions that should be addressed in the proposal. Full proposals are reviewed and analyzed by several staff members. Staff members meet to select a final group of proposals for consideration by the board of directors.

5. Decision by the board of directors. Staff prepare a "Recommendation for Grant Action" for each proposal. This document includes a summary of the need and problem being addressed, the applicant organization, project activities, project personnel, and budget. It also includes the staff's assessment of the reasons that the foundation should fund the project, as well as the risks. Board members ask staff to provide additional information, discuss the merits of the proposed projects and their relationship to the foundation's strategy, and either approve or disapprove the projects.

Hitachi Grant Review: An Example of a Nonfunded Proposal

PROJECT: A community-based organization requests $125,000 over 3 years to support the expansion of its work into 50 neighborhoods in Washington, DC. The organization works with low-income neighborhoods to help them invest in the future of their young people. The program involves developing locally created investment funds for scholarships, community service projects, new business opportunities, long-range planning, leadership development, and educational activities. Funds are requested to support leadership development, education, and public awareness activities in one major urban neighborhood. The proposal had the following strengths and weaknesses.

Strengths:
- This project/organization is highly consistent with the foundation's philosophy and approach in both education and community development.
- It works to link education and community development, relying on the wisdom and energy of local people to solve their own problems while building their skills and sense of pride.
- This project develops local leadership and involves many people and organizations in the education process.
- The project can stimulate other kinds of neighborhood development.
- The organization, and its dynamic young leader, have accomplished a great deal and have an excellent reputation in the community.

Weaknesses:
- The project relies heavily on the vision and leadership of *one* individual, without a sense for broader organizational capacity.
- The plans for expansion into 50 neighborhoods are too ambitious, given that the organization has worked in only six neighborhoods over the past 2½ years.

- It is hard to understand the substance and content of what the organization actually does in neighborhoods. What is the real impact of what they do?
- The organization needs to raise $3.5 million over the next 3 years to support expansion into 50 new sites. Given their list of current and potential funders, this goal is very unrealistic.

Other Questions:

1. How do they measure/evaluate their impact?
2. What is the substance of their "educational partnerships" and community service activities?
3. Are the programs in the six original neighborhoods ongoing? What is the role of local community people in maintaining them?
4. Beyond the energy and expertise of the organization's founder and director, how capable is the organization? What is the organization's reputation with local neighborhood groups?
5. They say that the program provides an opportunity for different people and groups to work together on issues beyond education, such as business development, health, and housing. Does this really happen? What are examples?
6. Why are they planning such a large expansion at this time? What training and skills does the organization need to succeed in expanding its program?
7. How will requested funds be used? What are the goals, objectives, desired outcomes, activities, and evaluation measures?

DECISION: Decline.

Hitachi Grant Review: An Example of a Funded Proposal

ORGANIZATION: First Nations Development Institute

PROJECT: Requests $76,295 over 1 year to support planning efforts related to the establishment of the First Nations Funders' Collaborative. The overall goal of the collaborative is to create sustainable, Indian-controlled economies on Indian reservations by (a) increasing the quality of economic development projects, (b) increasing the quantity of funding available to them, and (c) building the capacity of foundations and Indian communities to pursue such development. The collaborative will provide grant funds and technical assistance for Native American development projects and will engage in evaluation, policy advocacy, and dissemination activities. Funds are requested to design and implement the systems and to train the staff needed to effectively start and manage the collaborative. The reviewers found that the proposal had the following strengths and weaknesses.

Strengths:
- The time is right to launch such an initiative—there is a huge need as well as great interest among funders and Native American organizations in working together.
- First Nations Development Institute has an excellent reputation among Indians and others and is well positioned to undertake this project. The foundation also has a long funding history and positive relationship with the organization.
- The organization's approach to community development is consistent with the foundation's own approach to community building.
- The collaborative, and the planning process for which funds are requested, will (a) build the capacity of First Nations Development Institute to provide money and training to other Indian organizations; (b) help create a "philanthropic infrastructure," giving Indian groups access to foundations; (c) educate foundations on the needs and programs in "Indian Country"; and (d) provide a model for how grantmakers and grantseekers can work together effectively.
- Local and national Indian organizations are supportive of and involved in the project.
- The Hitachi Foundation seeks to leverage greater resources and has often done so by supporting the planning activities for larger initiatives.
- The project is national in scope, with the potential for great and long-term impact.

Weaknesses:
- In any collaborative effort, there exists the potential of creating another layer of bureaucracy, making it harder for community organizations to get the funds they need.

Questions:
1. What are the organizational implications for First Nations Development Institute? Will the collaborative replace its other activities?
2. What capacity needs to be built within the organization for it to successfully undertake this project?
3. How will First Nations be able to adjust to its new role as a funder? How will this role affect its ability to be successful in Indian communities?
4. What will be the role of other national Native American organizations?
5. Why is the planning phase so expensive?
6. What would be the foundation's role vis-à-vis other, larger foundations? What unique contribution will we be able to make?

DECISION: Grant awarded.

The collaborative has been launched, and the foundation is currently considering providing more grant funds for the activities of the collaborative.

Interviews

Interviews with people who award grants provide insights into what the funders are seeking. The two interviews here provide useful information about both the funding process and the development of winning proposals.

ROBERT FITZPATRICK, VICE PRESIDENT AND SECRETARY, PROCTER & GAMBLE

Procter & Gamble (P&G) is a significant donor to education in the United States. Between July 1992 and June 1993, P&G gave more than $10 million to fund kindergarten through graduate school programs. Included were contributions of $4,504,000 in grants to colleges and universities, $2,767,198 in matching gifts, $200,000 to the United Negro College Fund, $395,000 to public policy research, $247,200 to economic education organizations, and $180,000 to environmental organizations and projects. Engineering research and development and grants to colleges and universities totaled $5,186,000. Worldwide contributions made by P&G totaled $45,401,413.

In his tenure as Vice President and Secretary of the Procter & Gamble Fund, Cincinnati, Ohio, for the past 10 years, Mr. Robert Fitzpatrick has directed multimillions in grant placements. To assist the novice grantwriter, Mr. Fitzpatrick answered the following questions for this book.

P&G contributed $10 million in 1992 and 1993 to fund kindergarten through graduate school education. Does this fluctuate? What are the figures for K-12 education?
The sum P&G contributes to education doesn't vary much, but there is a slight upward trend by a small percentage per year. About 1 million dollars went to fund early life through K-12 education from P&G funds last year.

What education programs do you like to fund and to which would you give automatic priority?
We give preference to schools in areas where P&G has a large employee presence. That is, we are especially concerned about public education in areas such as Cincinnati, Ohio, where our U.S. headquarters is located, among others.

What is P&G's focus in its contributions strategy?
Procter & Gamble focuses on the comprehensiveness of the effort within areas such as Cincinnati, where we have developed a real ongoing partnership between business leaders and 34 public and private school districts, with an emphasis on the inner-city school community. The *entire school community* must be considered for desired changes to occur.
"The Cincinnati Youth Collaborative" has been a vital and effective force for change. P&G has 500 employees who volunteer in this project and in both public and private schools in the Cincinnati area on a regular basis. More than 2,000 P&G employees are social service volunteers in the Cincinnati community. We strongly support such employee volunteer efforts. The P&G Fund has also contributed to the National Alliance of Business for the development of a partnership with schools across the United States—an effort which is funded by a collaborative effort of U.S. corporations to support education reform efforts.

In P&G's contributions to schools, what are your funding priorities? What types of projects do you prefer to fund?

Projects which will result in *substantially fewer* dropouts, in *more* students receiving high school diplomas, and in *more* passing scores are important to us.

Do you have other funding priorities for school grants?

If schools meet other requirements, we would be interested in whether or not programs funded provide both parental instruction in the basics of effective parenting and external support for the working parent. Topics such as how to do homework with your kids and how to deal with touchy emotional issues should be covered.

I see that P&G contributes to the National Hispanic Scholarship Fund and the Leadership Conference on Civil Rights Education Fund. Are you interested in supporting minorities?

Yes. At this time we are making a special effort on behalf of all U.S. minorities. We are emphasizing more contributions to minority colleges and we are hiring more African Americans and other minorities.

P&G granted more than $4.5 million to colleges and universities in 1992-1993 dedicated to "our children and our future." How did you select these particular institutions?

P&G needs to have a continuous supply of qualified employees and leaders. Therefore, those 4-year institutions which supply our employees have first priority. A wide range of institutions across the United States is represented in this group.

What is the focus of your school improvement grants?

We take a holistic approach to improving entire neighborhoods as exemplified by the active participation of our senior executives in collaborative efforts such as The Business Roundtable. Bob Wehling, President of the P&G Fund, has provided leadership to The Roundtable in the development of its position on education reform. P&G takes the perspective that the school is simply one major entity within the entire community. [This is reflected by the $7,500 grant to the National Center for Neighborhood Enterprise.]

Which of the health and social service organizations which shared a total of $4,490,083 in 1992-1993 has received the larger share of grant monies?
P&G supports the United Way as the umbrella organization which, on the local level, meets community needs for social services.

What do you see as the major challenge to the provision of social services by the United Way and other agencies you support? And, can this impact school grants?
The major challenge is *getting people to work together.* We support efforts to *integrate* social services into the schools and have found that the United Way consistently attempts to accomplish this goal.

What do you see as the future trend in grant awards?
Field of Service Grants are the grants of the future. Procter & Gamble and its 22 subsidiaries each identify major needs within their communities, then ask their employees to help. Each asks of himself/herself, "How can I help?" Responses to this question generate programs in each area, frequently originating in local activity affiliated with the United Way.

What does this mean for teachers and administrators who need grant monies for challenging projects in which people are encouraged to work together?
They need to work together themselves. *Coalitions* of school districts should be developed to obtain grants. The broader the coalition, the better the chance for receiving funding. This is generally the rule.

Procter & Gamble has developed and distributed educational mate-
rials in the schools. Do you fund proposals related to this type of
project?
External projects of this type are limited. However, P&G has
funded *About Marketing* and *Planet Patrol,* home economics
and social studies materials which are available for the classroom.

What are some types of projects that might interest P&G in the near
future?
A major issue for Procter & Gamble is that of the environment. [Procter & Gamble awarded $180,000 to support envi-
ronmental projects from June 1992 to June 1993.] The disposal
of solid waste is a major concern. We are spending large sums
to be sure that our products have minimal negative impact on
the environment and would be interested in projects related
to this issue. I expect that early life, K-12 education, higher
education, and other social services will continue to be our
major focus. [In 1992-1993, P&G contributed large sums to
these programs: the Special Olympics, Caring Program for
Kids, Give Kids the World, City Kids Foundation, and Students Against Drunk Driving.]

What resources or reading materials do you recommend for addi-
tional insights into the grantseeking process?
John McNight's book, *Building Communities From the Inside*
Out, expresses the essential idea that many groups and institutions must work collaboratively to achieve success in turn-
ing around inner cities. Schools, churches, businesses, etc.,
must work in tandem for success. I also recommend an education publication of The Business Roundtable, *Primer for*
Business Involvement in Education. Business needs to be involved in both granting money for education projects and in
providing hands-on involvement with the educational process in schools.

TIP: Learn as much as possible about the screening proc-
ess of a potential funder!

MRS. ANN MANLEY, DIRECTOR OF THE
DR. PHILLIPS FOUNDATION

Mrs. Ann Manley, Executive Director of the Dr. P. Phillips Foundation, P.O. Box 3753, Orlando, Florida 32801, recommends that teachers and administrators follow some key guidelines in the grant search and application process. Approach the grant process with clarity and organize your application much as you would review a new education program in your school setting. That is, in your application for funding, provide the following essential information:

1. *The main purposes or goals of the grant.* Provide a comprehensive plan for the grant focusing on goals.
2. *Documentation of the problem.* Designate whom the grant will serve and why.
3. *A project budget.* Provide a simple budget for your project indicating requisite expenditures.
4. *Your plan for organization of grant components.* Indicate how activities will be organized as they relate to budget and administrative considerations.
5. *An evaluation plan.* Include your plan for evaluating the effectiveness of your project. Tell the funder how you plan to measure your success in meeting project goals.
6. *A plan to share information about your project.* Let the funder know how you will share information about your project within your school and with other educators. Do you have plans for articles to be placed in professional journals? If your plan includes press releases, will these be limited to local papers, or will nationally syndicated features be a part of the effort? If you have received other grants, authored publications, or received other awards or honors, provide documentation of these professional credentials in support of your grant application.

Site Visitations

If you receive a visit from a foundation representative, it will be preceded by a formal letter or phone call from your funder. A project may be selected for a site visit for several reasons.

1. It has become a serious candidate for funding, having been selected in the first stage(s) of the screening process.
2. Once funded, site visitations are part of the funder's oversight process for underwritten projects.
3. The project director might request such a visit as a step to obtaining additional dollars or technical services.
4. Problems have surfaced that require assistance by the funder.

Site visits are tools to assist you in improving the project and in meeting project goals.

The establishment of a close working relationship with the grantmaker is key to a successful project. Create a positive image in working with the funder and the funder's staff assistants at the beginning of the application process. Once rapport is established, make every effort to keep the funder informed about all important aspects of the work in progress. Personal contact with the funder on an informal but regular basis provides the opportunity to deal with a potential problem before it becomes a real problem.

Activities to Strengthen Grant Partnerships

Develop record-keeping goals for your project that are closely linked to monitoring goals, specific activities, and purposes expressed by the funder who has awarded you the grant. Discuss your plans for documenting grant activities with the funder. Obtain the funder's approval and input into the process. Strengthen opportunities for sustaining an ongoing dialogue with your funder on a regular basis. Build and support a collaborative venture that can overcome any unanticipated start-up difficulties. Even if no immediate obstacles are encountered in the implementation of your grant, friendly cooperation between you and the funder can provide positive, albeit unanticipated, side effects that will benefit your project. If yours is a project that has not been tried before, you will want to identify several critical points in the development of the process. Obtain the input of grantwriters who have successfully overcome such challenges. However, if you are proposing a large-scale project that is a first, consider limiting first steps to a smaller scale "pilot project." A pilot program has the advantage of smallness so that the director and staff can regulate factors, and the evaluation can closely monitor each aspect of your pilot. Seed monies for pilot projects are available from many foundations. Foundations that indicate preferences for funding projects that are broad in scope may consider a pilot project that is submitted as the first phase of a more comprehensive long-range innovation.

The Monitoring Process

The following describes the monitoring process implemented by the Hitachi Foundation to supervise grant activities. You will want to contact *each* grantmaker to identify the specific process used by that foundation to monitor grant recipients.

Monitoring of Grants: Objectives

1. To keep track of a project's progress and determine if grant funds are being used appropriately
2. To assist the grant recipient in improving the effectiveness of the project
3. To determine future opportunities for foundation action

Monitoring Activities

1. Review of written interim and final reports
2. Regular telephone conversations with project personnel
3. Site visits
4. Participation in grant recipient events
5. Review of evaluation plan and results
6. Review of budgets and financial statements
7. Provision of technical assistance

Principles of Good Monitoring

1. Build trust and mutual respect.
2. Establish realistic expectations and reporting requirements.
3. Be supportive and engage in problem solving and advising without interfering with project management.

4. Understand and pay attention to the project budget.
5. Maintain regular formal and informal communications with grant recipients.
6. Assist grant recipients to see the larger context within which their projects operate and to identify opportunities for expanding their impact.

In the planning stages, design a process that follows the guidelines and mandates of the funder. Administrative procedures should be structured and implemented to ensure that you are in compliance at all times with your funder's requirements. All expenditures are to be accounted for as per your agreement with the funder. Documentation of all grant activities, recorded and regularly updated, will prepare you for a site visit from a grantor.

TIP: *Emphasize the efficiency of your plan for record keeping and for the ongoing monitoring of your grant!*

Summary

Carefully examination of the interviews with funders and criteria for proposal scoring that were reviewed in this chapter can provide invaluable tools in helping you assess a wide range of possible proposal inclusions. Chapter 5 will provide information about state-funded grants for classrooms. Guidelines are presented for developing proposals to receive state grants for classroom improvement, and rating criteria for proposals are discussed. Resources that include contact information for small grants are also provided at the end of the book to help both the experienced and the novice proposal writer.

5

Grant Resources for
Teachers, Students, and Schools

Chapter Highlights

- State-Supported Grants
- Benefits of Proposal Development

Chapter 5 is intended for use by educators who are seeking small grants for a wide range of purposes. The chapter includes ideas for small research and development (R&D) projects that are state funded. Edited lists of sources of awards for small grants and for some awards from specific agencies are found in Resource B. This chapter is primarily focused on getting the first-time proposal writer aimed toward a successful start.

At this stage, ask and answer the questions posed in introductory chapters of this book. Review material presented on donor identification and donor contact. Obtain and appropriately complete grant applications from each potential funder, as suggested in earlier sections of this book, enhancing your proposal to meet both the funder's specific grant guidelines and the unique requirements of your project. Present all needed information effectively to make your case. Obtain detailed financial information from your agency or district, as requested by the funder, for accurate completion of the proposed budget. Enlist the support of essential others to assist in proposal development from the inception of the process. Included in this group may be your district superintendent, comptroller, school board members, parents, the business community, and other potential stakeholders.

To assist you in making a favorable impact on the proposal reader, present information about professional recognition you have received. Nominations for awards may be considered worthy of inclusion in your resumé. List successful collaborative projects that you have directed or with which you have been affiliated.

Before you begin collecting data to complete a grant application, review information about the projects recently funded by the grant-maker to be certain you have a good match. In this way, you may avoid wasting your time.

Expanding Funding Possibilities

If you do not yet have a substantial history of receiving grants and successful project work—a history that would provide evidence of your expertise as a principal investigator on a project—you may want to consider taking the preliminary step of seeking another type of award to get you started. Some of the same sources that fund grants to educators also make awards for excellence to teachers and to students for achievement. Your receipt of such an award or the winning of an achievement award by one of your students may provide an excellent starting point from which to gain the positive attention of the funder. Lists of sources of awards for teaching, student achievement awards, and school partnership incentives are presented in Resource B.

State-Supported Grant Options: Collaborative Research

Although relatively few teachers actually write grant proposals, there are ample opportunities for funding if teachers and others cooperate in useful and productive ways. For example, educators often decry the gaps among higher education, research, and use of research results to improve public schools. Simultaneously, researchers complain that teachers act like craftspeople, relying very little on the scientific evidence that recent research has produced. One way to hurdle this abyss is for teams of higher education personnel and local school-site persons to conduct cooperative research in schools. Junior faculty in higher education are especially eager to develop research agendas. They are logical candidates to help teachers design and conduct research action on educational practice in school sites. There are various sources of support for well-conceptualized projects of research on practice, and the collaboration that begins with a single-focus project has the potential for long-lasting cooperation that will expand the impact of each partner in the collegial enterprise.

For example, North Carolina has supported this sort of cooperative research with modest awards of funds (up to $10,000 per proposal) to higher education personnel to conduct research in school settings. The Small-Grants/School-Based Research Initiative, funded by the University of North Carolina Board of Governors, is open to any professor who plans to conduct, with representatives of the local school system, collaborative research in a school setting with a goal of education improvement. One operative word here is collaborative, or cooperative. No professor can submit a proposal that has not been developed cooperatively and reviewed by representatives at the participating school district and school building site where the research will occur. Projects typically run for about 1 year. Grant funds do not pay for such things as salaries for higher education personnel or indirect costs, charges that can consume much of a small grant's budget. Funds will support teacher in-service activities, data collection, data analysis and interpretation, test instrumentation and testing, design of questionnaires, support for typing help and research assistants, and other direct costs to operate the project. The proposal is limited to five pages (plus a cover form).

Although school improvement is the major desired outcome of this work, the nontechnical nature of the guidelines encourages even a novice researcher and proposal writer to apply—and that is another purpose of the awards program. A third purpose is to establish cooperative work between higher education (people who typically do research) and local school personnel (people who should do some research *and* who would use research results).

It is possible that such a school-based research effort may not provide funding precisely for the particular activity that you prefer to do. Yet often an area of primary interest might become a secondary activity in the research effort and thus get financial support. An example might be teacher in-service training as part of the treatment in the research endeavor. Paying for a treatment (e.g., training) as a part of a research project is a very legitimate expenditure. Although the funds go to the university applicant, cooperating teachers can benefit from this funding program by (a) working with higher education personnel so that the goals of both may be met through joint effort; (b) obtaining some training and classroom help, such as materials and other support; (c) learning about conducting action research; and (d) improving their grantseeking and proposal-writing skills through practice.

EXAMPLE OF STATE EDUCATION AGENCY GRANTS OPTIONS

State education agencies often offer opportunities for teachers to develop small, competitive proposals and secure some funding for projects in designated program areas. For example, South Carolina provides "mini grants" through its Education Improvement Act (EIA) funding. The state education agency invites teachers to develop small, easy-to-prepare proposals for limited funding; the projects support innovative teaching practices, including the purchase of some supplies and materials. Even in these small projects, however, the teacher must design some evaluation efforts, and this suggests cooperating with faculty in higher education who can help with the evaluation and data analysis.

The EIA "Grants to Improve Teaching Practices and Procedures" application format is similar to many other grantmaking approaches. The invitation to teachers to participate—often called the Request for Proposals, or RFP, process—presents an overview of the grants program.

The eight-page application provides three pages for cover page, signatures, and assurances, and five pages of boxed-in sections into which all information requested under each category must be placed. The proposal section headings are similar to those found in many grants competitions.

Project Summary
Problem Area
Goals and Objectives
Evaluation Plan
Description of Activities
Timeline

Exportable Product Description
Budget Breakdown

Although the example provided here is from one state-level grants program, it is not unlike opportunities available in other settings, including locally sponsored competitive grants either from a governmental source or from community or private sources. Proposals are competitive: You will not get the award unless you take some action to try to get the award.

Proposal Development as
Personal and Professional Growth

A proposal—a clear statement of needs, activities, outcomes, and costs—is a common way to plan and conduct business in society. Even if there is no specific plan to seeking funding, a good proposal is a clear statement of a person's understanding of a situation and what the person hopes to do. A proposal demonstrates both the person's knowledge and that person's plan to take some action.

Developing a proposal is a learning experience (in writing skills, problem identification and analysis, use of library research, etc.) and suggests a continuing quest for added knowledge. Active educator involvement in project development and action research not only provides content for a professional portfolio and opportunities for growth through presentations and writing, but it also leads to improvements in conducting the business of education. The development of a proposal demonstrates the writer's *personal commitment* to improvement because of the background work, writing, time, and cost that the person will devote to proposal development. Proposal development also demonstrates a writer's *professional commitment* as it will improve the writer's knowledge and the services that the writer or agency will provide to the clients. Because the tasks of a proposal will usually take added time and work, the agency's support and housing (including fiscal accountability) of the project demonstrate *institutional commitment* to the issues addressed in the proposal. Indeed, developing a proposal and managing the grant funds and project resulting from a successful proposal have both rewards and problems or pitfalls. Although this book is about finding funds and developing proposals to obtain external support, a brief listing of the rewards and problems of securing a grant may be useful.

Rewards of Securing a Grant and Project

Developing a proposal, receiving grant funds, and setting up a project do have some important rewards. The first reward is the actual completion of the proposal as a product of your own industry. There is intrinsic pleasure in successful competition.

A successful proposal offers you autonomy to try out your ideas and offers some flexibility from the usual "daily rut" or rat race. You may have extra help, funds for added material and supplies, chances to travel and network, and opportunities for personal and professional visibility and advancement. Successful projects offer you opportunities to disseminate your results through presentations and writings, and these situations will help you expand your own influence and range of acquaintances. Cooperation that you receive in operating your project may turn into successful and long-term collaboration.

When you combine the above rewards to the professional pleasure of improved practice and improved service to clients, the effort expended to obtain grant funding seems little price to pay. Yet not everything about obtaining funding is positive.

Problems and Pitfalls in Securing a Grant

Writing a proposal and getting it funded may seem, at first glance, to be all benefit and no problems. A wise philosopher once noted that a shingle, no matter how thin, still has two sides. A proposal writer should at least consider that one or more pitfalls may entrap the successful grant recipient.

1. Unless it is a project large enough to be your entire workload, managing the grant (proposal) may be just extra work with little or no extra pay. If you are a teacher on a 10-month contract, you might be able to secure an added month to pay for the grant-related effort. Usually, how-

ever, you just do the extra work (management, scheduling, record-keeping, evaluation, reports, etc.) for the pleasure of having your project and to reap the rewards discussed above. If you are skillful, you might get a clerk, teacher assistant, intern, or some consultant help.

2. You will be accountable for the funds and the appropriate management of the project.

3. There will be plenty of paperwork: reports, ordering, scheduling, letters, invoices, and so on.

4. You will now be serving two masters—your regular employer and the funding agency. This may be a problem at first, but intelligent management processes usually can relieve some of the pressure.

5. Records, records, records. Perhaps records come under the category "paperwork," but here also are files, accounts, samples of all work done, details of meetings (e.g., minutes or reports), and so on.

6. You will need to become thoroughly familiar with all of the administrative procedures to support an ongoing project: personnel, calendar, negotiated agreements, purchasing procedures, and so on.

7. Jealousy. Your colleagues will either congratulate you and work with you or act envious, even jealous, of your new-found autonomy and power. Just having a project and funding will alter some long-standing relationships. You may get news coverage and recognition and have opportunities to meet new people and discuss your project. Some grant winners put jealousy into the "Benefits" category above!

In many ways, obtaining a grant and managing the resulting project bring you full circle. You have learned a new skill (proposal development), you have made contacts (the funder), you have expanded your sphere of influence, and now you are part of a network, so you are an insider. You have demonstrated your ability to identify a problem and operate a project to solve the problem. You have income-generating capabilities and have enjoyed the benefits of your project. You may have learned new evaluation skills, human relations skills, and "politics."

It is a sure bet that you will try again. And when you do, you will be ahead of the novice because of the project that you just received.

Summary

In Chapter 5, information has been presented to assist you in locating information about available state-supported grants. Continue your exploration to answer specific questions about a potential funder or a grant in Resource B. Careful research can assist you in identifying earlier grant recipients who may be contacted for additional information. You may be surprised to discover two or more potential funders for your project. In this effort, you will find the grant libraries an invaluable resource. They are listed in Resource C.

Resource D presents information about foundations that provide support for innovation in education. Carefully review each source to see if there is a match between the funder's areas of interest and your project. Because these foundations are major players in education grant funding, use these resources creatively to ensure that your project has every chance of success.

Small Grant Opportunities

One way to get started in the proposal business is to apply for relatively small projects and for excellence awards. Many such opportunities exist, often through professional and honorary associations such as those listed in Resource A. Resource B provides examples of small grant funding opportunities.

Foundation Support for Education

The foundations in Resource D provide support for large-scale school improvement models. Although some of the foundations listed limit giving to regional applicants, many fund projects from qualified applicants anywhere in the United States. Source of foundation information is from filed IRS form 990-PF returns.

With few exceptions, based on tax incentives, foundations make awards solely to nonprofit organizations. In this group are the vast majority of public schools and school districts, and many private schools, as well as higher education institutions. Although there are some grants available for individuals, in most cases, the educational institution, not the individual teacher or administrator, is the grant applicant.

When you are determining whether or not a grantmaker might be an appropriate funder for your project, be creative in your approach. Consider collaborating with other educators, social service agencies, and/or area businesses. Design a comprehensive, long-range, and innovative program that could find a new solution to one of the old problems in our schools.

You might limit your initial plan to a pilot study to begin the project. Thus, you would need fewer dollars to implement your program. Formulate clear goals, a detailed activity plan and timeline, and a statistically sound evaluation plan for the project. Review the literature to identify successful models for what you are trying to accomplish. You will want to visit a library that has a complete foundation collection to review annual reports at these libraries for specific recipients, projects funded, and amount of awards.

In your activity plan, include some of the strategies that worked for the experts. You will want to collect baseline data for your evaluation design, describe your program, and assess its degree of effectiveness.

Develop a broad funding base for the project, including both contributions of dollars and in-kind contributions from business. The popularity of your project within the school community, added to the strong funding base from several sources that you are developing for your program, should enhance your ability to obtain foundation monies. Happy prospecting!

Resource A:
Professional Education Associations

1. American Association of Colleges for Teacher Education (AACTE), 1 Dupont Circle NW, Washington, DC 20036; (202) 293-2450.
2. American Association of Physics Teachers (AAPT), 5112 Berwyn Rd. #200, College Park, MD 20740; (301) 345-4200.
3. American Association of School Administrators (AASA), 1801 N. Moore St., Arlington, VA 22209; (703) 528-0700.
4. American Association of State Colleges and Universities, 1 Dupont Circle NW #700, Washington, DC 20036; (202) 293-7070.
5. American Association of University Women (AAUW), 1111 16th St. NW, Washington, DC 20036; (202) 785-7700.
6. American Council on Education (ACE), 1 Dupont Circle NW #800, Washington, DC 20036; (202) 939-9300.
7. American Educational Research Association (AERA), 1230 17th St. NW, Washington, DC 20036; (202) 223-9435.
8. American Federation of Teachers (AFT), 555 New Jersey Ave. NW, Washington, DC 20001; (202) 879-4400.
9. American Library Association (ALA), 50 E. Huron St., Chicago, IL 60611; (312) 944-6780.
10. American Psychological Association, 1200 17th St. NW #200, Washington, DC 20036; (202) 955-7600.
11. American Society for Training and Development, Alexandria, VA, 1640 King St., Alexandria, VA 22314; (703) 683-8100.
12. American Sociological Association (ASA), 1722 N St. NW, Washington, DC 20036; (202) 833-3410.
13. Association for Supervision and Curriculum Development (ASCD), 225 North Washington St., Alexandria, VA 22314; (703) 549-9110.
14. Association for the Care of Children's Health, 7910 Woodmont Ave. #300, Bethesda, MD 20814; (301) 654-6549.

15. Council for Basic Education, 725 15th St. NW #801, Washington, DC 20005; (202) 347-4171.
16. Council for Educational Development and Research, 1201 16th St. NW, Washington, DC 20036; (202) 223-1593.
17. Council for Exceptional Children, 1920 Association Dr. #121, Reston, VA 22091; (703) 620-3660.
18. Council of Great City Schools, 1413 K St. NW #400, Washington, DC 20005; (202) 371-0163.
19. Council on Foundations, 1828 L St. NW, Washington, DC 20036; (202) 466-6512.
20. Mathematical Association of America (MAS), 1529 18th St. NW, Washington, DC 20036; (202) 387-5200.
21. Music Educators National Conference, 1902 Association Dr., Reston, VA 22091; (703) 860-4000.
22. NAFS: Association of International Educators, 1875 Connecticut Ave. NW #1000, Washington, DC 20036; (202) 462-4811.
23. National Alliance of Black School Educators, 2816 Georgia Ave. NW, Washington, DC 20001; (202) 483-1549.
24. National Art Education Association, 1916 Association Dr., Reston, VA 22091; (703) 860-8000.
25. National Association for the Education of Young Children (NAEYSC), 1834 Connecticut Ave. NW, Washington, DC 20009; (202) 232-8777.
26. National Association of Elementary School Principals (NAESP), 1615 Duke St., Alexandria, VA 22134; (703) 684-3345.
27. National Association of Partners in Education, 209 Madison Ave. #401, Alexandria, VA 22314; (703) 836-4880.
28. National Association of Secondary School Principals (NASSP), 1904 Association Dr., Reston, VA 22091; (703) 860-0200.
29. National Council for Social Studies, Washington, D.C., 3501 Newark St. NW, Washington, DC 20016; (202) 966-7840.
30. National Education Association (NEA), 1201 16th St., Washington, DC 20036; (202) 833-4000.
31. National Geographic Society, 1145 17th St. NW, Washington, DC 20036; (202) 857-7000.
32. National School Boards Association, 1680 Duke St., Alexandria, VA 22314; (703) 838-6277.
33. National School Public Relations Association, 1501 Lee Hwy. #2101, Arlington, VA 22209; (703) 528-5840.
34. National Science Teachers Association (NSTA), 1840 Wilson Blvd., Arlington, VA 22209; (703) 243-7100.
35. Overseas Education Association, 1201 16th St. NW, Washington, DC 20036; (202) 822-7850.
36. Phi Delta Kappa (PDK), P.O. Box 789, Bloomington, IN 47402-0789; (812) 339-1156.

Resource B:
Selected Listing of
Small Grant Opportunities

Sources for Classroom-Level and Small Grants

1. Academic Alliance Awards, Southern Regional Education Board, c/o J. Triplett, 592 10th St. NW, Atlanta, GA 30318-5790. Matching-funds grant limited to selected areas. Obtain guidelines.
2. Annenberg/CPB Math and Science Project, Attn: Guidelines, Initiative I or II, 901 E St. NW, Washington, DC 20004-2006. Grants for supplies to enhance needed changes in science education.
3. Business Week Awards, c/o Charlotte Frank, Vice President, Research and Development, Macmillan/McGraw-Hill, 20th Fl., 1221 Avenue of the Americas, New York, NY 10020. Grants for classroom innovations.
4. Chrysler Family Reading Grants, c/o Andrea Wood, Chrysler Learning Corporation, 500 N. Michigan Ave., Chicago, IL 60611. Grants for implementing new and creative programs that involve families in reading. Grants are one-time, nonrenewable awards.
5. Continental Cablevision, Pilot House, Lewis Wharf, Boston, MA 02210. Classroom awards for projects that use distance learning, video production, or multimedia in conjunction with "Cable in the Classroom" television programming.
6. Expeditionary Learning, Outward Bound USA, 122 Mount Auburn St., Cambridge, MA 02138. Grants for projects that extend learning to the outdoors.
7. Highsmith Research Grants, American Library Association, c/o Marie-Louise Settem, 50 E. Huron St., Chicago, IL 60611. Grants for individuals to research student learning and libraries.

8. Lifetouch Enrichment Awards, Lifetouch National Schools Studios, Inc., 7800 Picture Drive, Minneapolis, MN 55439-3148. Grants for classroom projects. Guidelines are available.
9. National Council of Teachers of English, NCTE Research Foundation, 1111 Kenyon Rd., Urbana, IL 61801. Grants for classroom-based research and for collaborative projects. Applicants must be members of NCTE.
10. National Society for Experiential Education, 3509 Haworth Dr., Suite 207, Raleigh, NC 27609-7229.
11. NCSS Geography Grant, 3501 Newark St. NW, Washington, DC 20016. Awards to grant proposals that enhance geographic literacy—for all teachers involved in social studies education.
12. NFIE Student Success Grants, NFIE, 1201 Sixteenth St. NW, Washington, DC 20036. Grants for creating, implementing, and administering successful and innovative projects aimed at at-risk students.
13. Serve America, Youth Community Service Projects, Florida Department of Education, Suite 414, 325 West Gaines St., Tallahassee, FL 32399-0400. Grants are for projects that develop student volunteer programs. Florida residents.
14. Teaching Peace Program, Peace Development Fund, 44 North Prospect St., P.O. Box 270, Amherst, MA 01004.

Scholarships for Academic Leave or Independent Research

1. AFT International Affairs Department, 555 New Jersey Ave. NW, Washington, DC 20001. American Federation of Teachers opportunity for teaching in newly democratized countries of Russia and Eastern Europe. Requirements vary depending on program and country.
2. Carroll Preston Baber Research Grant, American Library Association, Office of Research and Statistics, 50 E. Huron St., Chicago, IL 60611. Grant is awarded to the best proposal for research on the improvement of library services; open to librarians and teachers who are ALA members.
3. Fulbright Full Grants, U.S. Student Programs Division, Institute Plaza, New York, NY 10017.
4. Fulbright Teacher Exchange Program, Attn. TMA, 600 Maryland Ave. SW, Rm. 235, Washington, DC 20024-2520. Teacher exchange with an overseas teacher for 1 year.
5. Harvard World Teach, Philips Brooks House, Harvard University, Cambridge, MA 02138. Two-year commitments required; volunteer work in developing and/or newly democratized countries.
6. James Madison Memorial Fellowship Program, P.O. Box 4030, Iowa City, IA 52243-4030. Fellowships fund expenses of a master's degree in American history or political science. Focus on the U.S. Constitution.

7. Kellogg National Fellowship Program. Info: P.O. Box 5196, 180 South Union St., Battle Creek, MI 49017. A 3-year award program designed to provide professionals with opportunities to develop leadership capabilities in the early years of their careers. Involves grantees in a variety of interdisciplinary study activities. Mission: To develop "better informed, more creative (leaders) who are better suited to the needs of a changing, diversified society." A basic goal of the Kellogg Program is "to assist future leaders in developing skills and competencies which transcend traditional disciplinary and professional methods of addressing problems." Program scope: 50 grants to individuals of up to $35,000 for 3-year period. Additional funds for travel expenses. Advantages: Fellows continue employment with nonprofit employer. Employer receives reimbursement of 12.5% of Fellow's salary, up to aggregate of $32,000. Employer must provide release time.
8. National Fellowships for Independent Study in the Humanities, Council for Basic Education, P.O. Box 135, Ashton, MD 20861. For K-12 teachers. Fellowship enables teachers to conduct independent research for 1 year.
9. NEH Teacher-Scholar Program for Elementary and Secondary School Teachers, Division of Education Programs, National Endowment for the Humanities, 1100 Pennsylvania Ave. NW, Washington, DC 20506.
10. Newberry Library Awards Committee, 60 W. Walton St., Chicago, IL 60610-3380. Numerous awards of varying sizes available for 6 to 11 months of research in any subject related to the Newberry Library Collection. Stipends accompany awards.
11. The A. Verville Fellowship at the Smithsonian's National Air and Space Museum, c/o Fellowship Coordinator, National Air and Space Museum, MRC 313, Washington, DC 20560. One-year fellowships for research in residence at the Smithsonian Museums and the Library of Congress. Fellows work in conjunction with staff from the Department of Aeronautics.

Some Grants From American Association of University Women (AAUW)

1. American Fellowships—Awarded to support doctoral and postdoctoral study by women. Selection criteria: Scholarly excellence, teaching experience, active commitment to helping women through community service, profession, and/or interest field. Three grant categories are offered: (a) postdoctoral fellowships, (b) dissertation fellowships, and (c) postdoctoral research. Contact AAUW for additional information.
2. Career Development Grants—For women in early stages of academic studies to reenter the workforce, change careers, or advance current careers. Purpose: To assist women in achieving career goals. Requirement: Applicants must enroll in courses at accredited colleges, technical schools, or university programs that are prerequisites to professional employment plans. Doctoral

candidates receive coursework (no dissertation) funding. Preference: Given to AAUW members, women of color, women pursuing first terminal degree, and women pursuing nontraditional field degrees. Funds for tuition, fees, books, supplies, local transportation, and dependent care. Fellowship stipend: $1,000-$5,000. Apply by mid-December. Contact funder for details.

3. Community Action Grants—Provides seed money to AAUW branches, state associations, or individual women for nondegree research projects that promote education or equity for women. Grant range: $500-$5,000.

4. International Fellowships—For full-time graduate study, postgraduate study, or research in the United States and other countries. Selection criteria: Applicants with outstanding academic ability and equivalent of BA by application date. Preferences to women in origin countries. Six of 42 fellowships sponsored by the International Association of University Women reserved for affiliate members. Fellowship stipend: $15,065. December 1 application deadline.

5. Teacher Fellowships—The Eleanor Roosevelt Fellowships awarded to female public school teachers with at least three consecutive years of full-time teaching experience. Purpose: To help enrich classroom teaching, encourage professional development, and broaden educational opportunities for women and girls, with a focus on math, science, and technology. Requirements: Applicant must be a U.S. citizen or permanent resident and teach full-time at a U.S. public school in Grades K-12. Must teach math, science, or technology as part of teaching assignment. Fellowship stipend: $1,000-$10,000. Obtain applications by December for early January deadline.

Numerous funders of small grants to classroom teachers also offer academic achievement awards to students. If your students have received such awards, do not forget to cite this information on your resumé and other accompanying grant application materials to help make your case.

Funding Opportunities for Students

1. AAUW, P.O. Box 4030, Iowa City, IA 52243-4030. American Association of University Women offers awards for female students in mathematics and science.

2. Air Afrique/Gessler Essay Contest, Gessler Publishing Company, 55 West 13th St., New York, NY 10011. Open to secondary French students; prize is an expense-paid trip to Senegal, Africa.

3. American Express Student Geography Awards, P.O. Box 672227, Marietta, GA 30067. Awards for students in Grades 6-12 who design and complete intensive geography projects.
4. Ann Arlys Bowler Poetry Prize, Weekly Reader Corporation, 245 Long Hill Rd., Middletown, CT 06457. U.S. Savings Bonds awarded to middle and secondary students.
5. Brooks Brothers Scholars Program, c/o Coopers & Lybrand, P.O. Box 4620, Grand Central Terminal, New York, NY 10163. College scholarships available to high school seniors.
6. DuPont Challenge Science Essay Awards Program, General Learning Corporation, 60 Revere Dr., Northbrook, IL 60062-1563. Cash prizes and expense-paid trips to the space center in Houston, TX.
7. The Freedom Forum, c/o Karen Catone, 1101 Wilson Blvd., Arlington, VA 22209. Open to high school seniors who are planning to major in journalism at a 4-year U.S. college.
8. National Awards Contest for Cursive Handwriting, Peterson Directed Handwriting, 315 S. Maple Ave., P.O. Box 249, Greensburg, PA 15601-0249. Open to students in Grades 3 through 8.
9. "National Geographic World," Splash Contest, Catherine Hughes, Box 37357, Washington, DC 20013-7357. Open to students K-9 who are asked to create a radio announcement about the importance of fresh water.
10. National Nutrition Teen Video Contest, Florida Dept. of Citrus, 2755 E. Oakland Pk. Blvd., Ft Lauderdale, FL 33306. Teens write, direct, and star in music videos that they create about nutrition. Prizes include expense-paid trips to Universal Studios and cash awards.
11. NEH Younger Scholars Award, Division of Fellowships and Seminars, 1100 Pennsylvania Ave. NW, Washington, DC 20506. Summer stipend to study with a teacher mentor, who also receives a nominal stipend.
12. NHRA Youth and Education Services, 2035 Financial Way, Glendora, CA 91740. Scholarships from Sears and the National Hot Rod Association. Open to high school seniors for automotive technology careers.
13. Seiko Youth Challenge, DRB Communications, 1234 Summer St., Stamford, CT 06905. Open to teams of students in Grades 9-12 to identify and investigate a community environmental problem and come up with a solution. Scholarships and cash prizes are awarded.
14. Skirball Institute on American Values, c/o Ruthy Thabb, 635 Harvard Blvd., Suite 214, Los Angeles, CA 90005-2511. Cash prizes for winning essays on an American value that can be documented in the nation's history.
15. Speak for Yourself Letter-Writing Contest, 625 4th Ave., S. Minneapolis, MN 55415. Open to students in Grades 7 and 8. Sponsored by RespecTeen.
16. Tylenol/NASSP Launch Essay Contest. Applications are available at retail stores selling Tylenol, or by writing to NASSP, 1904 Association Dr., Reston, VA 22091. Prizes awarded for best student essays on ideas for school-level projects. Cash prizes are awarded to students and schools.

17. Union Mastercard Scholarships, P.O. Box 907, Minneapolis, MN 55440-0907. Undergraduate college scholarships for UTD members, their spouses, and children.
18. Westinghouse Science Talent Search, 1719 N St. NW, Washington, DC 20036. Open to scientifically gifted high school seniors; prizes include scholarships and expense-paid trips to Washington, DC.
19. The Write Stuff, Call (800) 822-9762. Works of fiction, nonfiction, photography, cartoons, poetry, and so on are submitted for possible publication by students in Grades 7 through 12. Call for additional information.
20. Young Playwrights Festival, Dept. PR, 321 West 44th St., Suite 906, New York, NY 10036. Winners have their plays produced; staged readings of others are presented.

The preceding list of funding sources is a start to help you find support for those students who may be creative and eligible for an award. Awards of this sort are evidence of your superior work with students.

Awards for Excellence in Teaching

In making your case for grant support, it is important to note on your resumé and other materials you submit to a funder any recognition for excellence in teaching you have received. Professional awards may enhance the presentation of the proposal writer as an "expert" and may be essential in effectively making your case. Furthermore, many of the companies that fund grants to educators also make "excellence in teaching awards."

1. A&E Cable Network, Community Development, P.O. Box 1610, Grand Central Station, New York, NY 10163. A&E Cable Network Awards for teachers who have developed network programs and/or videos.
2. American Association for Library Service to Children (ALSC) Distinguished Service Award, c/o ALA, 50 E. Huron St., Chicago, IL 60611.
3. Black Entertainment Cable Network (BET), 1700 N. Moore St., Suite 2200, Rosslyn, VA 22209. Awards for teachers who have developed lessons based on selected BET Programs.
4. Catalyst Awards, c/o Director, CMA, 2501 M St. NW, Washington, DC 20037. Chemical Manufacturers Association offers the program to honor outstanding middle and high school chemistry teachers.
5. Defense of Academic Freedom Award, NCSS, 3501 Newark St. NW, Washington, DC 20016. Award recognizes an individual who has made a contribution to preservation of academic freedom in social studies education.

6. Distinguished Dissertation in Teacher Education Award, c/o Gerald Krockover, Purdue University School of Education, 1443 Matthews Hall, Rm. 106, West Lafayette, IN 47907-1443. Award honors doctoral-level research on teacher education.

7. Eleanor M. Johnson Award; Nila Banton Smith Award, International Reading Association, P.O. Box 8139, Newark, DE 19714-8139.

8. Excellence in Indian Education Awards, NASF, 8200 Mountain Rd. NE, Suite 203, Albuquerque, NM 87110. Native American Scholarship Fund awards; open to teachers or schools serving Indian students.

9. Geraldine Dodge Celebration of Teaching Program, Box 1239, Morristown, NJ 07962-1239. Fifty awards to teachers for essays on ways to encourage students to seek teaching careers.

10. Geraldine Dodge Curriculum Design Awards, CLASS, 39 Main St., Geneseo, NY 14454. Awards given for innovative curricula in mathematics and language arts; Grades 7-12.

11. Gruber and Heidi Castleman Awards for Excellence in Chamber Music Teaching, Chamber Music America, 545 8th Ave., New York, NY 10018. Awards open to teachers who bring chamber music experience into their classrooms.

12. Gustav Ohaus Award, NSTA Awards Programs, 1840 Wilson Boulevard, Arlington, VA 22201-3000. K-12 to improve science teaching.

13. Hollingworth Award Committee, 4300 Sideburn Rd., Fairfax, VA 22030-3507. Supports research on the education and psychology of gifted youth.

14. The Kohl International Teaching Awards, Dolores Kohl Education Foundation, 165 Green Bay Road, Wilmette, IL 60091. For K-12 teachers. Join the Kohl International Academy of Outstanding Educators.

15. National Awards for Teaching Economics, NCEE and IPCF, 432 Park Ave. South, New York, NY 10016. Awards for innovative curricula in economics; K-12.

16. National Principal-of-the-Year Award, NASSP, 1904 Association Dr., Reston, VA 22091-1537. Awards open to school leaders with at least 3 years of experience; candidates must be nominated and must be members of NASSP at the time of selection.

17. National Teachers Hall of Fame, 1320 C of E Dr., Emporia, KS 66801. Five awards per year; winners are honored by the U.S. President at a White House reception.

18. Optical Data Videodisc Awards, c/o Sherry Greenshields, (800) 248-8478, Ext. 2164. K-12—awards for teacher-developed activities using videodiscs.

19. Phillips Petroleum Environmental Partnership Awards, Phillips Petroleum Co., 16D1 PB, Bartlesville, OK 74004. Awards for science teachers—K-12.

20. Polymer Education Coordinator, Miami University at Middletown, 4200 E. University Blvd., Middletown, OH 45042. Award for excellence in polymer education by a middle or secondary chemistry teacher.

21. Presidential Awards for Excellence in Science and Mathematics Teaching, NSTA Special Projects, 3140 N. Washington Blvd., Arlington, VA 22201. K-12—two teachers selected each year.
22. Reader's Digest American Heroes in Education Awards, Reader's Digest, Reader's Digest Road, Pleasantville, NY 10572.
23. Robert Foster Cherry Awards, Baylor University, 500 Speight, Waco, TX 76798-7412. Two awards—The Robert Foster Cherry Chair for Distinguished Teaching and the R.F. Cherry Award for Great Teachers.
24. Sallie Mae First-Year Teacher Award, c/o Nancy C. Murphy, Student Loan Marketing Association, 1050 Thomas Jefferson St. NW, Washington, DC 20007. Awards for outstanding first-year teachers. Superintendent must nominate the teacher.
25. Spirit of America Award, National Council for the Social Studies, 3501 Newark St. NW, Washington, DC 20016. Award recognizes educational contributions that exemplify the American democratic spirit.
26. Tandy Technology Scholars Program, P.O. Box 32897, TCI Station, Ft. Worth, TX 76129.
27. Writer's Digest Writing Competition, Writer's Digest, 1507 Dana Ave., Cincinnati, OH 45207. Awards for articles, short stories, poems, or scripts.

Phi Delta Kappa Awards

Phi Delta Kappa (PDK) has 43 scholarships for school students (seniors) who plan to become teachers. Forty-two are for $1,000. One is for $2,000. Cut-off date is January annually. Procedure is to contact your local PDK Chapter for application forms. These are available after October 1 annually. Four scholarships are designated for minority students. Two are set aside for children of Kappans. For members of PDK, there are five awards for graduate study. Two of these are for $1,500 for doctoral students who are full-time students. PDK members who have been accepted into a doctoral degree program may apply. Two of them are $500 research stipends for PDK members who have earned doctoral degrees. One $750 award is reserved for a PDK member who is a full-time master's degree student. The deadline for application on the Howard M. Soule Scholarship Program is May 1 annually. Applications are available after January 1 from your local PDK Chapter. Or contact the PDK headquarters (see Resource A).

Partnership Awards

School/business partnerships are increasingly important in providing dollars for classroom projects. Selected sources of awards for successful partnerships are listed here.

1. The American Bar Association (ABA) recognizes outstanding partnership efforts that serve the public. Annually cash grants totalling $20,000 are provided by Information America, an Atlanta-based company. Education partnerships are included in the award categories. Contact Roseanne Lucianek, Director, Center for Partnership Programs, ABA, 541 N. Fairbanks Ct., Chicago, IL 60611-3314, (312) 988-5464, for more information.
2. The Greenville Foundation gives primarily in Washington State, Oregon, California, and Arizona for local programs; but it also gives both nationally and internationally, providing small classroom grants to teachers for innovative classroom projects. The Greenville Foundation has funded the Los Angeles Educational Partnership. Contact California Community Foundation, 606 S. Olive St., Suite 2400, Los Angeles, CA 90014, for more information.
3. The Lilly Endowment is supporting the Algebra in Middle Schools Project, Dorchester, MA, in the amount of $604,018 for the expansion of the project to help middle school students make the transition from arithmetic to algebraic concept. Lilly primarily supports projects within its region of the United States. Contact the Lilly Foundation at 2801 N. Meridian St., Indianapolis, IN 46208.
4. U.S. West Foundation funds projects in their 16 service areas and recently earmarked $103,928 for a four-state teacher project to use technology to develop classroom materials and curricula. Contact U.S. West for grant guidelines at 7800 East Orchard Rd., Suite 300, Englewood, CO 80111, (303) 793-6661.

National Science Teachers Association (NSTA) Awards

The National Science Teachers Association (NSTA) offers a variety of awards, including cash and prizes for its "best and brightest" science educators and students. Information about NSTA awards may be obtained by writing to. NSTA Awards Programs, 1840 Wilson Boulevard, Arlington, VA 22201-3000.

1. Access Excellence. Sponsor: Genentech, Inc. Eligibility: High school biology teachers (Grades 9-12). One hundred high school biology teachers actively participate in the on-line Access Excellence Forum and share classroom activities and learn about current scientific developments through connections to working scientists and other experts. Awards: A trip to San Francisco for training on the network, a laptop computer, and free access to America Online. Deadline: mid-January, annually.
2. AGA-STAR (Science Teaching Achievement Recognition) Awards. Sponsor: American Gas Association. Eligibility: K-12 and college/university

science educators. This program offers awards to teachers to implement or continue a novel idea or approach aimed at improving science education at the precollege and university levels. Awards are given in two categories: precollege level and college or university level. Awards: three awards of $1,000, $750, and $500 in each category. Deadline: November 15, annually.

3. American Water Works Association Award. Sponsor: American Water Works Association. Eligibility: K-12 science teachers. This award recognizes a precollege teacher who has developed an instructional program and/or innovation that encourages minority students to study and enjoy science in association with drinking water. Award: $1,000 and up to $500 toward expenses to attend the NSTA National Convention. Deadline: November 15, annually.

4. CIBA-GEIGY Elementary Principal Award. Sponsor: CIBA-GEIGY Corporation (Conducted by the Council for Elementary Science International, an NSTA affiliate). Eligibility: Elementary principals. Focus: Innovative leadership and design of an outstanding elementary science program. Awards: $1,000, 1-year NSTA and CESA membership, and up to $500 for national conference attendance. Deadline: November 15, annually.

5. CIBA-GEIGY Exemplary Elementary Science Teaching Award. Sponsor: CIBA-GEIGY Corporation (conducted by the Council for Elementary Science International, an NSTA division affiliate). Eligibility: Full-time elementary science teachers. The award is given to an elementary science teacher who has demonstrated exemplary science teaching practices in one or more of the following areas: creating science materials; using science materials; designing teaching plans and ideas; and fostering student, school, and school-community instructional programs in science. Award: $1,000, 1-year membership in CESI and NSTA, and up to $500 to attend NSTA's National Convention. Deadline: November 15, annually.

6. NSTA/TAPESTRY. Toyota Appreciation Program for Excellence to Science Teachers Reaching Youth. Year-long grants support innovative science education.

7. STAR (Science Teaching Achievement Recognition) Awards, NSTA. Awards to K-12 and university educators who have created a novel approach to precollegiate science education; program must have been implemented prior to application date.

8. Toshiba Exploravision Science Program, c/o Pamela Riley, Program Manager, Toshiba/NSTA Exploravision Award. Awards available to students in K-12. Write for information.

Vocational and Career Education Grants

Regional grants are awarded for career or vocational education by the following selected foundations. These are limited to particular localities. Contact foundations directly for additional information.

ALABAMA

J. L. Bedsole Foundation, AmSouth Bank, N.A., P.O. Box 1628, Mobile, AL 36629. Grants for capital support.

DISTRICT OF COLUMBIA

Morris and Gwendolyn Cafritz Foundation, 1825 K St. NW, 14th Fl., Washington, DC 20006. Funds vocational programs in carpentry and related trades.

ILLINOIS

Lloyd A. Fry Foundation, 135 S. LaSalle St., Suite 1910, Chicago, IL 60603. Funds model teacher training programs at vocational high schools.

MASSACHUSETTS

Jessie B. Cox Charitable Trust. Info: Grants Management Associates, 230 Congress St., 3rd Fl., Boston, MA 02110. Funds health centers in vocational and middle schools.

MICHIGAN

Charles Stewart Mott Foundation, Office of Proposal Entry, 1200 Mott Foundation Bldg., Flint, MI 48502-1851. Funds school-to-work transition programs for vocational high school students.

MINNESOTA

General Mills Foundation, P.O. Box 1113, Minneapolis, MN 55440. Funds vocational programs in culinary arts.

MISSOURI

Ewing Marion Kauffman Foundation, 4900 Oak, Kansas City, MO 64112. Funds business and technology high school programs in Missouri.

NEW JERSEY

Allied Signal Foundation, 101 Columbia Rd., P.O. Box 2245, Morristown, NJ 07962-2245. Awards to school-to-work partnerships in areas of company operations.

NEW YORK

Louis Calder Foundation, 2320 Park Ave., Rm. 1530, New York, NY 10169. Grants in New York area for computer simulations for high school students.

Aaron Diamond Foundation, 1270 Avenue of the Americas, Suite 2624, New York, NY 10020. New York City high schools receive awards for technology courses.

Greenwall Foundation, Two Park Ave., 23rd Fl., New York, NY 10016. National awards for vocational and technical high school students.

Charles Hayden Foundation, One Bankers Trust Plaza, 130 Liberty St., New York, NY 10006. Grants to Boston, New York, and New Jersey areas for vocational high school programs.

Margaret L. Wendt Foundation, 40 Fountain Plaza, Suite 277, Buffalo, NY 14202-2220. Support for technical high schools in western New York state.

PENNSYLVANIA

Connelly Foundation, One Tower Bridge, #1450, West Conshohocken, PA 19428. Awards to Philadelphia and Delaware Valley to high schools for vocational education programs.

RHODE ISLAND

Champlin Foundations, 410 S. Main St., Providence, RI 02903. Grants to Rhode Island vocational-technical centers.

TEXAS

Cooper Industries Foundation, First City Tower, Suite 4000, P.O. Box 4446, Houston, TX 77210. Support in Houston and areas of company operations for vocational education centers.

WISCONSIN

Faye McBeath Foundation, 1020 N. Broadway, Milwaukee, WI 53202. Awards to Wisconsin area for vocational technical schools for at-risk youth.

Resource C:
Libraries With
Foundation Grant Collections

Four reference collections are operated by the Foundation Center, an independent national service organization sponsored by foundations. Each has a complete set of U.S. foundation IRS returns (IRS Form 990-PF) on file.

Foundation Center Reference Collections

1. The Foundation Center, 79 Fifth Ave., 8th Fl., New York, NY 10003, (212) 620-4230.
2. The Foundation Center, 312 Sutter St., Rm. 312, San Francisco, CA 94108, (415) 397-0902.
3. The Foundation Center, 1001 Connecticut Ave. NW, Washington, DC 20036, (202) 331-1400.
4. The Foundation Center, Kent H. Smith Library, 1422 Euclid, Suite 1356, Cleveland, OH 44115, (216) 861-1933.

Other Reference Libraries With Foundation Collections

The following libraries, listed by state, have regional or state IRS returns (IRS Form 990-PF) on file for area foundations.

121

ALABAMA

Auburn University at Montgomery, Library, 7300 University Dr., Montgomery, AL 36117-3596, (205) 244-3653.

Birmingham Public Library, Government Documents, 2100 Park Place, Birmingham, AL 35203, (205) 226-3600.

ALASKA

University of Alaska at Anchorage, Library, 3211 Providence Dr., Anchorage, AK 99508, (907) 786-1848.

ARIZONA

Phoenix Public Library, Business & Sciences Unit, 12 E. McDowell Rd., Phoenix, AZ 85004, (602) 262-4436.

Tucson Pima Library, 101 N. Stone Ave., Tucson, AZ 87501, (602) 791-4010.

ARKANSAS

Westlark Community College, Borham Library, 5210 Grand Ave., Ft. Smith, AR 72913, (501) 785-7133.

CALIFORNIA

California Community Foundation, Funding Information Center, 606 S. Olive St., Suite 2400, Los Angeles, CA 90014-1526, (213) 413-4042.

Nonprofit Center Development Library, 1762 Technology Dr. #225, San Jose, CA 95110, (408) 452-8181.

Peninsula Community Foundation, Funding Information Library, 1700 S. El Camino Real, R301, San Mateo, CA 94402-3049, (415) 358-9392.

Santa Barbara Public Library, 40 E. Anapamu St., Santa Barbara, CA 93101, (805) 962-7653.

San Diego Community Foundation, Funding Information Center, 101 West Broadway, Suite 1120, San Diego, CA 92101, (619) 239-8815.

Ventura County Community Foundation, Funding & Information Resource Center, 1355 Del Norte Rd., Camarillo, CA 93010, (805) 988-0196.

COLORADO

Denver Public Library, Social Sciences & Genealogy, 1357 Broadway, Denver, CO 80203, (303) 640-8870.

CONNECTICUT

Hartford Public Library, 500 Main St., Hartford, CT 06103, (203) 293-6000.

DELAWARE

University of Delaware, Hugh Morris Library, Newark, DE 19717-5267, (302) 451-2432.

FLORIDA

Jacksonville Public Libraries, Business Science & Documents, 122 N. Ocean St., Jacksonville, FL 32202, (904) 630-2665.

Miami-Dade Public Library, Humanities/Social Science, 101 W. Flagler St., Miami, FL 33130, (305) 375-5575.

Nova Southeastern University, Einstein Library, 3301 College Ave., Ft. Lauderdale, FL 33314, (305) 475-7050.

Orlando Public Library, Social Sciences Dept., 101 E. Central Blvd., Orlando, FL 33801, (407) 425-4694.

Tampa-Hillsborough Group Public Library, 900 N. Ashley Dr., Tampa, FL 33602, (813) 213-8865.

GEORGIA

Atlanta-Fulton Public Library, Foundation Collection-Ivan Allen Department, 1 Margaret Mitchell Square, Atlanta, GA 30303-1089, (404) 730-1900.

HAWAII

Hawaii Community Foundation, Hawaii Resource Center, 222 Merchant St., 2nd Fl., Honolulu, HI 96822, (808) 537-6333.

University of Hawaii, Hamilton Library, 2550 The Mall, Honolulu, HI 96822, (808) 956-7214.

IDAHO

Boise Public Library, 715 S. Capitol Blvd., Boise, ID 87302, (208) 384-4024

Caldwell Public Library, 1010 Dearborn St., Caldwell, ID 83605, (208) 459-3242.

ILLINOIS

Donors Forum of Chicago, 53 W. Jackson Blvd., Suite 430, Chicago, IL 60604-3608, (312) 431-0265.

Evanston Public Library, 1703 Orrington Ave., Evanston, IL 60201, (708) 866-0305.

Sangamon State University Library, Shepherd Rd., Springfield, IL 62794-9243, (217) 786-6633.

INDIANA

Allen County Public Library, 900 Webster St., Ft. Wayne, IN 46802, (219) 424-0544.

Indianapolis-Marion County Public Library, Social Science Department, 40 W. St. Clair, Indianapolis, IN 46206, (317) 269-1733.

IOWA

Cedar Rapids Public Library, Foundation Collection, 500 First St. SE, Cedar Rapids, IA 52401, (319) 398-5123.

Public Library of Des Moines, 100 Locust, Des Moines, IA 50309-1791, (515) 283-4152.

Southwestern Community College, Learning Resource Center, 1501 W. Townline Rd., Creston, IA 50801, (515) 782-7081.

KANSAS

Topeka and Shawnee County Public Library, 1515 W. 10th St., Topeka, KS 66604, (913) 233-2040.

Wichita Public Library, 223 S. Main St., Wichita, KS 67202, (316) 262-0611.

KENTUCKY

Louisville Free Public Library, 301 York St., Louisville, KY 40203, (502) 561-8617.

LOUISIANA

East Baton Rouge Parish Library, Centroplex Branch Grants Collection, 120 St. Louis, Baton Rouge, LA 70802, (504) 389-4960.

New Orleans Public Library, Business & Science Division, 219 Loyola Ave., New Orleans, LA 70140, (504) 596-2580.

Shreve Memorial Library, 424 Texas St., Shreveport, LA 71120-1523, (318) 226-5894.

MAINE

University of Southern Maine, Office of Sponsored Research, 246 Deering Ave., Rm. 628, Portland, ME 04103, (207) 780-4871.

MARYLAND

Enoch Pratt Free Library, Social Science & History, 400 Cathedral St., Baltimore, MD 21201, (301) 396-5430.

MASSACHUSETTS

Associated Grantmakers of Massachusetts, 294 Washington St., Suite 840, Boston, MA 02108, (617) 426-2606.

Boston Public Library, Humanities Reference, 666 Boylston St., Boston, MA 02117, (617) 363-5400.

Worcester Public Library, Grants Resource Center, Salem Square, Worcester, MA 01608, (508) 799-1655.

MICHIGAN

Alpena County Public Library, 211 N. First St., Alpena, MI 49797, (517) 356-6188.

Battle Creek Community Foundation, Southwest Michigan Funding Resource Center, 2 Riverwalk Centre, 34 W. Jackson St., Battle Creek, MI 49017-3505, (616) 962-2181.

Farmington Community Library, 32737 West 12 Miles Rd., Farmington Hills, MI 48018, (313) 553-0300.

Grand Rapids Public Library, Business Department, 3rd Fl., 60 Library Plaza NE, Grand Rapids, MI 49503-3093, (616) 456-3600.

Henry Ford Centennial Library, Adult Services, 16301 Michigan Ave., Dearborn, MI 48126, (313) 577-6424.

Michigan State University Library, Social Sciences/Humanities Main Library, East Lansing, MI 48824-1048, (517) 353-8818.

Michigan Technological University, Van Pelt Library, 1400 Townsend Dr., Houghton, MI 49931, (906) 487-2507.

Northwestern Michigan College, Mark & Helen Osterin Library, 1701 E. Front St., Traverse City, MI 49684, (616) 922-1060.

Sault Ste. Marie Area Public Schools, Office of Compensatory Education, 460 W. Spruce St., Sault Ste. Marie, MI 49783-1874, (906) 635-6619.

University of Michigan—Ann Arbor, Graduate Library, Reference & Research Services Department, Ann Arbor, MI 48109-1205, (313) 664-9373.

University of Michigan Library—Flint, Flint, MI 48502-2186, (313) 762-3408.

Wayne State University, Purdy/Kresge Library, 5265 Cass Ave., Detroit, MI 48202, (313) 577-6424.

MINNESOTA

Duluth Public Library, 520 W. Superior St., Duluth, MN 55802, (218) 723-3839.

Minneapolis Public Library, Sociology Department, 300 Nicollet Mall, Minneapolis, MN 55401, (612) 372-6555.

MISSISSIPPI

Jackson-Hinds Library System, 300 N. State St., Jackson, MS 39201, (601) 968-5803.

MISSOURI

Clearinghouse for Midcontinent Foundations, University of Missouri, 5110 Cherry St., Kansas City, MO 64113-0680, (816) 235-1176.

Kansas City Public Library, 311 E. 12th St., Kansas City, MO 64111, (816) 221-9650.
Metropolitan Association for Philanthropy, Inc., 5615 Pershing Ave., Suite 20, St. Louis, MO 63112, (314) 361-3900.
Springfield-Greene County Library, 397 E. Central, Springfield, MO 65802, (417) 869-9400.

MONTANA

Eastern Montana College Library, Special Grants Collection, 1500 North 30th St., Billings, MT 59101-0298, (406) 657-1662.
Montana State Library, Library Services, 1515 E. 6th Ave., Helena, MT 59620, (406) 444-3004.

NEBRASKA

University of Nebraska—Lincoln, Love Library, 14th & R Streets, Lincoln, NE 68588-0410, (402) 472-2848.
W. Dale Clark Library, Social Sciences Department, 215 S. 15th St., Omaha, NE 68102, (402) 444-4826.

NEVADA

Las Vegas-Clark County Library District, 833 Las Vegas Blvd. North, Las Vegas, NV 89101, (702) 382-5280.
Washoe County Library, 301 S. Center St., Reno, NV 89501, (702) 785-4010.

NEW HAMPSHIRE

New Hampshire Charitable Fund, One South St., Concord, NH 03302-1335, (603) 225-6641.
Plymouth State College, Herbert H. Lamson Library, Plymouth, NH 03264, (603) 535-2258.

NEW JERSEY

New Jersey State Library, Governmental Reference Services, 185 West State St., Trenton, NJ 08625-0520, (609) 292-6220.

NEW MEXICO

New Mexico State Library, Information Services, 325 Don Gaspar, Santa Fe, NM 87503, (505) 827-3824.

NEW YORK

Buffalo & Erie County Public Library, History Department, Lafayette Square, Buffalo, NY 14203, (716) 858-7103.

Levittown Public Library, 1 Bluegrass Lane, Levittown, NY 11756, (516) 731-5728.

New York State Library, Humanities References, Cultural Education Center, Empire State Plaza, Albany, NY 12230, (518) 474-5355.

Onondaga County Public Library, 447 S. Salina St., Syracuse, NY 13202-2494, (315) 448-4636.

Rochester Public Library, Business, Economics & Law, 115 South Avenue, Rochester, NY 14604, (716) 428-7328.

White Plains Public Library, 100 Martine Ave., White Plains, NY 10601, (914) 422-1480.

NORTH CAROLINA

Asheville-Buncombe Technical Community College, Learning Resources Center, 340 Victoria Rd., Asheville, NC 28801, (704) 254-4960.

The Duke Endowment, 200 S. Tryon St., Suite 1100, Charlotte, NC 28202, (704) 376-0291.

State Library of North Carolina, Government & Business Services, Archives Bldg., 109 E. Jones St., Raleigh, NC 27601, (919) 733-3270.

Winston-Salem Foundation, 310 W. 4th St., Suite 229, Winston-Salem, NC 27101-2889, (919) 725-2382.

NORTH DAKOTA

North Dakota State University Library, Fargo, ND 58105, (701) 237-8886.

OHIO

Dayton & Montgomery County Public Library, 215 E. Third St., First Fl., East Side, Dayton, OH 45402, (513) 227-9500 x 211.

Public Library of Cincinnati & Hamilton County Grants Resource Center, 800 Vince St., Library Square, Cincinnati, OH 45202-2071, (513) 369-6940.

Toledo-Lucas County Public Library, Social Sciences Department, 325 Michigan St., Toledo, OH 43624-1614, (419) 259-5245.

OKLAHOMA

Oklahoma City University, Dulaney Browne Library, 2501 N. Blackwelder, Oklahoma City, OK 73106, (405) 521-5072.

Tulsa City-County Library, 400 Civic Center, Tulsa, OK 74103, (918) 596-7944.

OREGON

Multnomah County Library, Government Documents, 801 SW Tenth Ave., Portland, OR 97205, (503) 248-5123.

Pacific Non-Profit Network, Grant Resources Library, 33 N. Central, Suite 211, Medford, OR 97501, (503) 779-6044.

PENNSYLVANIA

Carnegie Library of Pittsburgh, Foundation Collection, 4400 Forbes Ave., Pittsburgh, PA 15213-4080, (412) 622-3114.
Free Library of Philadelphia, Regional Foundation Center, Logan Square, Philadelphia, PA 19103, (215) 686-5423.

RHODE ISLAND

Providence Public Library, 150 Empire St., Providence, RI 02906, (401) 521-7722.

SOUTH CAROLINA

Charleston County Library, 404 King St., Charleston, SC 29403, (803) 723-1645
South Carolina State Library, 1500 Senate St., Columbia, SC 29211, (803) 734-8666.

SOUTH DAKOTA

South Dakota State Library, 800 Governors Drive, Pierre, SD 57501-2294, (605) 773-5070, (800) 592-1841 (SD Residents).

TENNESSEE

Knox County Public Library, 500 W. Church Ave., Knoxville, TN 37902, (615) 862-5843.
Memphis & Shelby County Public Library, 1850 Peabody Ave., Memphis, TN 38104, (901) 725-8877.

TEXAS

Amarillo Area Foundation, 700 First National Place, 801 S. Fillmore, Amarillo, TX 79101, (806) 376-4521.
Community Foundation of Abilene, Funding Information Library, 500 N. Chestnut, Suite 1509, Abilene, TX 79604, (915) 676-3883.
Corpus Christi State University Library, Reference Department, 6300 Ocean Drive, Corpus Christi, TX 78412, (512) 994-2608.
Dallas Public Library, Urban Information, 1515 Young St., Dallas, TX 75201, (214) 670-1487.
El Paso Community Foundation, 1616 Texas Commerce Building, El Paso, TX 79901, (915) 533-4020.
Funding Information Center, 530 McCullough, Suite 600, San Antonio, TX 78212-8270, (210) 227-4333.
Funding Information Center of Fort Worth, Texas Christian University Library, 2800 S. University Dr., Ft. Worth, TX 76129, (817) 921-7664.
Hogg Foundation for Mental Health, Will C. Hogg Bldg., Rm. 301, Inner Campus Dr., University of Texas, Austin, TX 78713, (512) 471-5041.

Houston Public Library, Bibliographic Information Center, 500 McKinney, Houston, TX 77002, (713) 236-1313.

UTAH

Salt Lake City Public Library, 209 East 500 South, Salt Lake City, UT 84111, (801) 524-8200.

VERMONT

Vermont Department of Libraries, Reference & Law Information Services, 109 State St., Montpelier, VT 05609, (802) 828-3268.

VIRGINIA

Hampton Public Library, 4207 Victoria Blvd., Hampton, VA 23269, (804) 727-1312.

Richmond Public Library, Business, Science & Technology, 101 East Franklin St., Richmond, VA 23219, (814) 780-8223.

Roanoke City Public Library System, Central Library, 706 S. Jefferson St., Roanoke, VA 24016, (703) 981-2477.

WASHINGTON

Seattle Public Library, Social Sciences, 1000 Fourth Ave., Seattle, WA 98104, (206) 386-4620.

Spokane Public Library, Funding Information Center, West 811 Main Ave., Spokane, WA 99201, (509) 838-3364.

WEST VIRGINIA

Kanawha County Public Library, 123 Capitol St., Charleston, WV 25304, (304) 343-4646.

WISCONSIN

Marquette University Memorial Library, Foundation Collection, 1415 W. Wisconsin Avenue, Milwaukee, WI 53233, (414) 288-1515.

University of Wisconsin—Madison, Memorial Library, 728 State St., Madison, WI 53701, (608) 262-3242.

WYOMING

Laramie County Community College, Instructional Resource Center, 1400 E. College Drive, Cheyenne, WY 82007-3299, (307) 778-1206.

Natrona County Public Library, 307 E. 2nd St., Casper, WY 82601-2598, (307) 237-4935.

Resource D:
Foundations That
Support Educational Innovation

Aetna Foundation, Inc., 151 Farmington Ave., Hartford, CT 06156-3180, (203) 273-6382.

Assets (yr. ended 12/90): $40,393,110 (M).

Grants: $9,073,170; average: $500-$25,000.

Purposes and activities: To help preserve a viable society by supporting programs and organizations that can have a real impact on solving social problems and by providing support that will stimulate other donors. Priority areas of giving are problems of urban public education, minority higher education, improving minority youth employment opportunities, urban neighborhood revitalization, and so on. Contact funder for more information.

Fields of interest: Urban development, urban affairs, community development, education, education—minorities, higher education, educational associations, literacy, leadership development, youth, employment, minorities, housing, law and justice, performing arts, disadvantaged, AIDS, international affairs, and insurance education.

Types of support: Matching funds, employee matching gifts, employee-related scholarships, scholarship funds, special projects, annual campaigns, and renovation projects.

Limitations: Giving limited to U.S. organizations. No grants to individuals, no private secondary schools or religious purposes.

Application information: Application form required for FOCUS grants, Dollars for Doers, and Matching Gifts.
Initial approach: Letter with proposal summary.
Deadline: None.
Write: Diana Kinosh, Management Information Supervisor.

The George I. Alden Trust, c/o Rackemann, Sayer, & Brewster, P.O. Box 351, Boston, MA 02101, (617) 654-3321.
Assets (yr. ended 9/91): $5,819,188 (M).
Grants: 17 grants: $220,925 ($2,000-$25,000).
Purposes and activities: Grant support directed toward organizations providing care and administering to the needs of children who are blind, retarded, disabled, or who are either mentally or physically ill or organizations engaged in medical and scientific research directed toward the prevention or cure of diseases and disabilities particularly affecting children.
Fields of interest: Child development, child welfare, the handicapped, medical research, higher education, and elementary education.
Types of support: Research, seed money, and special projects.
Limitations: Giving primarily in Massachusetts. No grants to individuals.
Application information: Application guidelines.
Initial approach: Letter.
Write: William B. Tyler, State Street Bank & Trust Co.

American Honda Foundation, P.O. Box 2205, Torrance, CA 90509-2205, (310) 781-4090.
Assets (1992): $15,501,074 (M).
Grants (1990-93): Total awarded to youth, education, scholarships, and teaching: $4,689,682 (60%); math and science: $2,188,277 (27%); environmental grants: $81,667 (1%); social concerns: $523,207 (7%); mentally/physically challenged: $253,500 (3%); and job training grants: $121,903 (2%).
Purpose and activities: National associations working in youth and scientific education, including private and elementary and secondary schools, public and private colleges and universities, scholarship and fellowship programs, and scientific and educational organizations.

Fields of interest: Science and technology, youth, physical sciences, AIDS, secondary education, higher education, language and literature, disadvantaged, and social sciences.

Types of support: Scholarship funds, fellowships, special projects, seed money, operating budgets, general purposes, continuing support, and matching funds.

Limitations: No grants to individuals. Only to nonprofits.

Application information: Application form required.

Initial approach: Letter or telephone.

Deadlines: November 1, February 1, May 1, and August 1.

Write: Kathryn A. Carey, Manager.

The Annenberg Foundation, St. Davids Center, 150 Radnor-Chester Rd., Suite A-200, St. Davids, PA 19087.

Assets (7/91): $1,302,778,581 (M).

Grants: 171: $54,551,660 ($250-$9,020,000); average: $25,000-$50,000.

Purposes and activities: Supports efforts to advance the public well-being through improved communication. Encourages development of more effective ways to share ideas and knowledge. Support primarily for early childhood and K-12 education.

Fields of interest: Education, early childhood, elementary education, secondary education, and cultural programs.

Types of support: Seed money and special projects.

Limitations: No grants to individuals or for basic research, capital construction, or general operating expenses.

Application information: Published application guidelines.

Initial approach: Letter.

Write: Dr. Mary Ann Meyers, President.

The Benedict Foundation for Independent Schools, 607 Lantana Lane, Vero Beach, FL 32963.

Assets (yr. ended 12/91): $1,978,241 (M).

Grants: 6 grants: $67,500 ($10,000-$12,500).

Purposes and activities: Support primarily for independent secondary schools that are members of the National Association of Independent Schools for 10 consecutive years. Challenge grants are preferred for purposes of improving academic programs, scholarship aid, building programs, faculty salaries, faculty summer workshops, or other programs to improve the quality of the school's educational activities.

Fields of interest: Education and secondary education.

Types of support: Scholarship funds, building funds, and matching funds.

Limitations: No grants to individuals, or for endowment funds or operating costs; no loans.

Application information: Application form required.

Initial approach: Letter requesting application; six copies of proposal.

Deadline: Receipt of applications between January 1 and March 31.

Write: Mrs. Nancy H. Benedict, VP.

Stephen and Mary Birch Foundation, Inc., 501 Silverside Rd., Suite 13, Wilmington, DE 19809.

Assets (yr. ended 12/90): $101,328,851 (M).

Grants: 51 grants: $2,116,215 ($500-$770,000); average: $10,000-$100,000.

Purposes and activities: Emphasis on health agencies, youth agencies, social services, cultural programs, hospitals, and the blind.

Fields of interest: The handicapped, youth, health services, hospitals, cultural programs, social services, and civic affairs.

Application information: No application required.

Initial approach: Letter.

Deadline: None.

Write: Elfriede Looze.

Helen Brach Foundation, 55 W. Wacker Dr., Suite 701, Chicago, IL 60601, (312) 372-4417.

Assets (3/91): $56,040,936 (M).

Grants: 247 grants: $2,438,248; average: $5,000-$25,000.

Purposes and activities: Support for social and family services, including programs for the prevention of cruelty to children and child welfare, the homeless and housing, the aged, youth, women, the disabled and disadvantaged; secondary, higher, and other education; prevention of cruelty to animals; museums; health; and hospitals.

Types of support: Annual campaigns, building funds, equipment, general purposes, operating budgets, publications, renovation projects, research, and special projects.

Limitations: No grants to individuals.
Application information: Application form required.
Initial approach: Letter.
Write: Raymond F. Simon.

The Morris and Gwendolyn Cafritz Foundation, 1825 K St. NW, 14th Fl., Washington, DC 20006, (202) 223-3100.

Assets (yr. ended 5/1): $187,803,268 (M).

Grants: 230 grants: $9,893,780; average: $10,000-$50,000.

Purposes and activities: Giving only for programs of direct assistance, with emphasis on education, community service, arts and humanities, and health.

Fields of interest: Arts, cultural programs, education, education— minorities, performing arts, health, AIDS, drug abuse, social services, youth, disadvantaged, the aged, the homeless, hospices, housing, women, community development, and volunteerism.

Types of support: Operating budgets, continuing support, seed money, matching funds, scholarship funds, fellowships, and general purposes.

Limitations: Giving limited to greater Washington, DC area. No grants to individuals.

Application information: Application form not required.

Initial approach: Proposal.

Deadlines: July 1, November 1, and March 1.

Write: Martin Atlas, President.

The Annie E. Casey Foundation, One Lafayette Place, Greenwich, CT 06803, (203) 661-2773.

Assets (yr. ended 12/91): $666,840,353 (M).

Grants: 59 grants: $23,660,353; average: $5,000-$2,500,000.

Purposes and activities: Exclusively for disadvantaged children and their families. Emphasis on foundation-developed initiatives that raise public awareness of the status of children, reform major systems of service delivery, demonstrate innovative and effective service delivery, and affect public policy.

Fields of interest: Child welfare, youth, family services, delinquency, disadvantaged, public policy, law and justice, education, education—minorities, employment, leadership development, mental health, and social services.

Types of support: Technical assistance, special projects, conferences and seminars, and research.

Limitations: No grants to individuals.

Application information: The foundation supports a limited number of proposals that are consistent with the foundation's mission and strategies.

Write: Douglas W. Nelson, Executive Director.

The Chatlos Foundation, Inc., P.O. Box 915048, Longwood, FL 32791-5048, (407) 862-5077.

Assets (yr. ended 12/90): $81,486,782 (M).

Grants: 205 grants: $2,592,371; average: $1,000-$25,000.

Purposes and activities: Grants for higher education, including religious education and religious associations; giving also for hospitals, health agencies, social services, international relief, and child welfare.

Fields of interest: Education, higher education, religious schools, theological education, religion—Christian, hospitals, health, social services, the homeless, hunger, nursing, international relief, and child welfare.

Types of support: Operating budgets, emergency funds, equipment, land acquisition, matching funds, scholarship funds, special projects, publications, renovation projects, and student aid.

Limitations: No support for the arts. No grants to individuals, or for seed money, deficit financing, building or endowment funds, research, or conferences; no loans.

Application information: Only one grant to an organization within a 12-month period. Application form not required.

Initial approach: Letter or proposal.

Deadline: None.

Write: William J. Chatlos, President.

Chrysler Corporate Giving Program, 12000 Chrysler Drive, Highland Park, MI 48288-1919, (313) 956-5194. Mailing Address: P.O. Box 1919, Detroit, MI 48288.

Total giving: (yr. ended 12/90): $9,500,000: $5,500,00 grants and $4,000,000 for in-kind gifts.

Purposes and activities: Support for education, especially secondary education; leadership development, including Junior Achievement;

employment training; economic development; minority affairs; and community funds. Chrysler also has an asset donation program in which the corporation donates vehicles and auto parts to high schools and vocational schools for the training of auto mechanics and technicians.

Fields of interest: Education, arts, youth, minorities, higher education, secondary education, economics, crime and law enforcement, drug abuse, minority education, and vocational education.

Types of support: Equipment, donated products, operating budgets, employee volunteer services, in-kind gifts, special projects, continuing support, fellowships, emergency funds, matching funds, and employee-related scholarships.

Limitations: Giving primarily in major operating areas.

Application information: Application guidelines.

Initial approach: Letter to headquarters.

Write: Ms. Lynn A. Feldhouse, Administrator.

Chrysler Corporation Fund (same address as above).

Assets (yr. ended 12/91): $17,000,000 (M).

Grants: 1,098 grants: $9,552,529; average: $1,000-$50,000.

Purposes and activities: Supports community funds, education, cultural programs, and health and human services.

Types of support: Special projects, scholarships. Others.

Limitations: No support for primary or secondary schools.

Write: Ms. Lynn A. Feldhouse, Mgr.

Jessie B. Cox Charitable Fund, c/o Grants Management Assoc., 230 Congress St., 3rd Fl., Boston, MA 02110, (617) 426-7172.

Assets (12/90): $51,000,000 (M).

Grants: 87 grants: $3,077,976; average: $20,000-$50,000.

Purposes and activities: Grants for education, health, the protection of the environment, and the development of philanthropy. The trustees tend to favor organizations that have *not received prior grants,* and new approaches over those similar to previously funded projects; fixed amount of approximately $3 million to be paid out annually through the life of the trust.

Fields of interest: Education, higher education, environment, conservation, and health.

Types of support: Seed money and special projects.

Limitations: Giving primarily in New England. No religious support. Other exclusions.

Application information: Application form not required.

Initial approach: Brief concept paper, telephone call, or proposal.

Deadlines: January 15, April 15, July 15, and October 15.

Write: Michealle Larkins, Foundation Assistant.

The Arthur Vining Davis Foundation, 645 Riverside Ave., Suite 520, Jacksonville, FL 32204, (904) 359-0670.

Assets (12/90): $111,190,000 (M).

Grants: 79 grants: $4,992,000 ($5,000-$300,000).

Purposes and activities: Support largely for private higher education, hospices, health care, public television, and graduate theological education.

Types of support: Building funds, continuing support, endowment funds, equipment, fellowships, internships, land acquisition, matching funds, professorships, research, capital campaigns, general purposes, lectureships, operating budgets, publications, renovation projects, special projects, and technical assistance.

Limitations: Giving limited to the United States and its possessions and territories. No publicly funded institutions, no grants to individuals; no loans.

Application information: See annual report for information. Application not required.

Initial approach: Letter.

Deadline: None.

Write: Max Morris, Executive Director.

Digital Equipment Corporate Giving Program, 111 Powdermill Rd., Maynard, MA 01754-1418, (508) 493-9210.

Financial data (yr. ending 12/90): $37,000,000, including $31,000,000 for grants.

Purposes and activities: On a worldwide basis, "to improve the quality of life and encourage active employee participation in those communities in which we conduct business; to promote solutions to critical challenges facing the company and community; to help people develop the skills needed to support industrial growth and productivity; to encourage and promote equal access for all citizens; [and] to promote advances in technical and scientific knowledge."

Fields of interest: Israel, higher education, arts, health, civic affairs, humanities, youth, hospitals, cultural programs, education—minorities, environment, the handicapped, secondary education, Europe, Asia, AIDS, science, and technology.

Types of support: Research, scholarship funds, matching funds, employee matching gifts, employee-related scholarships, and donated products.

Limitations: Giving primarily in Digital operating areas worldwide, including the United States, Europe, Asia, and Israel. No grants for endowments or political activities.

Application information: Informational brochure (including application guidelines). Application form not required.

Initial approach: Letter and proposal.

Deadline: None.

Write: Jane Hamel, Corporate Contribution Manager.

The Educational Foundation of America, 35 Church Lane, Westport, CT 06880, (203) 226-6498.

Assets (yr. ended 12/90): $98,517,440.

Grants: 88 grants: $4,305,063; average: $10,000-$15,000.

Purposes and Activities: Grants primarily for education, arts, the environment, and medical sciences; giving also for higher education, including education for American Indians, medical education and medical research, children's education, and gerontological research.

Fields of interest: Education and secondary education.

Types of support: General purposes, operating budgets, continuing support, seed money, professorships, internships, scholarship funds, matching funds, special projects, research, publications, and fellowships.

Limitations: No grants to individuals. No capital or endowment funds. No loans.

Application information: Application form not required.

Initial approach: Letter.

Deadline: None.

Write: Diane M. Allison, Executive Director.

Exxon Educational Foundation, 225 East John W. Carpenter Freeway, Irving, TX 75062-2298, (214) 444-1104.

Assets (12/31/91): $15,583,000 (M).

Grants: 237 grants: $8,137,102 ($1,000-$1,200,000).

Purposes and activities: To aid education in the United States (a) by matching gifts to Exxon employees and retirees to colleges and universities; (b) by supporting college and university schools, programs, and departments making outstanding educational contributions in science, technology, and business; (c) by aiding organizations and associations serving significant segments of the educational community; and (d) through project-oriented mathematics programs in kindergarten through graduate school levels; undergraduate remedial education; and elementary and secondary school restructuring and teacher education reform, particularly as they relate to enhancing the success of the educational system with disadvantaged minority students.

Types of support: Employee matching gifts, general purposes, and special projects.

Limitations: No grants to individuals or for institutional scholarships or fellowships; no loans or renovation projects. Contact funder for other exclusions.

Application information: Applications only accepted for Mathematics Education Program. Contact foundation before submitting application. See published annual report and application guidelines.

Write: E .F. Ahnert, Executive Director.

First Interstate Bank of Arizona, N.A., Charitable Foundation, P.O. Box 29743, Phoenix, AZ 85038-9743, (602) 229-4544.

Assets: $3,714,490 (M).

Grants (1991): 270 grants ($100-$250,00); average: $500-$10,000.

Fields of interest: Youth programs, higher education, literacy, libraries, secondary education, adult education, minority education, health, AIDS, drug abuse, the homeless, and youth community development.

Types of support: Scholarship funds, seed money, capital campaigns, special projects, renovation projects, emergency funds, and equipment.

Limitations: Giving to Arizona-based organizations or national organizations that fund programs in Arizona. No individual, religious, endowment, or multiyear grants. No loans.

Application information: Application form required.

Initial approach: Letter.

Deadlines: Submit proposals January through June, September, and October.
Write: Dianne Stephens, Secretary.

Ford Motor Company Fund, The American Road, Dearborn, MI 48121, (313) 845-8711.
Assets (as of 1/1/92): $40,853,762 (M).
Grants: 1,456 grants: $20,028,448; average: $1,000-$25,000.

Purposes and activities: Support for education, including matching gifts for higher education and basic research grants; community funds and urban affairs; hospitals; and cultural programs.

Fields of interest: Education, higher education, community funds, urban affairs, hospitals, AIDS, cultural programs, and civic affairs.

Types of support: Matching funds, research, annual campaigns, publications, continuing support, conferences and seminars, equipment, employee scholarships, and employee matching gifts.

Limitations: Giving primarily in areas of company operations nationwide, with special emphasis on Detroit, MI. No grants to individuals, for building funds, scholarships, or fellowships.

Application information: Application form not required. Annual report, application guidelines, and informational brochure available.
Initial approach: Letter.
Deadline: None.
Board meeting dates: April and October.
Final notification: 6 months.
Write: Leo J. Brennan, Jr., Executive Director.

Charles A. Frueauff Foundation, Inc., 307 East Seventh Ave., Tallahassee, FL 32303, (904) 561-3508.
Assets (yr. ended 12/90): $69,410,662 (M).
Grants: 152 grants: $3,288,440; average: $10,000-$25,000.

Purposes and activities: Support for welfare services to children, mental health and other health services, hospitals, the indigent, the handicapped, and higher education, including student aid.

Fields of interest: Higher education, health, hospitals, mental health, health services, welfare, child welfare, and the handicapped.

Types of support: Operating budgets, annual campaigns, emergency funds, building funds, equipment, endowment funds, scholarship funds, matching funds, general purposes, continuing support, capital campaigns, and renovation projects.

Limitations: Giving limited to United States. No grants to individuals or for research; no loans.

Application information: Application form not required.

Initial approach: Proposal, telephone, or letter.

Deadline: March 31. Submit proposal between September and March.

Write: David A. Frueauff, Secretary.

Gates Foundation, 3200 Cherry Creek South Dr., Suite 630, Denver, CO 80209-3247, (303) 722-1881.

Assets (1/91): $95,411.

Grants: 103 grants: $4,165,403; average: $5,000-$25,000.

Purposes and activities: To promote the health, welfare, and broad education of mankind whether by means of research, grants, publications, the foundation's own agencies and activities, or through cooperation with agencies and institutions already in existence.

Fields of interest: Youth leadership development, humanities, cultural programs, historic preservation, social services, education, and civic affairs.

Types of support: Continuing support, building funds, capital campaigns, endowment funds, matching funds, renovation projects, special projects, equipment, fellowships, general purposes, land acquisition, and publications.

Limitations: Giving limited to company, except for foundation-initiated grants. No support for private foundations or individuals.

Application information: Application form not required.

Initial approach: Telephone.

Deadlines: January 15, April 1, July 15, October 15.

Write: Thomas Stokes, Executive Director.

General Electric Foundation, 3135 Easton Turnpike, Fairfield, CT 064431, (203) 373-3216.

Assets (yr. ended 12/90): $15,359,675 (M).

Grants: 443 grants: $14,735,889; average: $5,000-$100,000.

Purposes and activities: Institutional grants primarily in support of education, with emphasis on (a) strengthening specific areas of work in undergraduate education; (b) graduate-level research and teaching; (c) support for disciplinary fields, including the physical sciences, engineering, computer science, mathematics, industrial management, and business administration; (d) support for minority group education programs, with emphasis on engineering and business; and (e) matching educational contributions of employees and retirees. Support also for community funds in communities where the company has a significant presence, selected public schools, arts and cultural centers, public issues research and analysis, equal opportunity, international understanding, and other special grants. Grants are directed toward specific programs authorized by the trustees, and most are approved in advance of each calendar year.

Fields of interest: Higher education, educational associations, educational research, education—minorities, business education, physical sciences, engineering, science and technology, computer sciences, mathematics, urban affairs, community funds, arts, cultural programs, public policy, intercultural relations, civil rights, and AIDS.

Types of support: Annual campaigns, continuing support, employee matching gifts, fellowships, general purposes, publications, research, scholarship funds, seed money, and special projects. Limitations: Giving limited to the United States; grants to community funds limited to areas where GE has a significant presence. No giving to individuals or to religious groups; no loans.

Application information: Application form not required.
Initial approach: Proposal.
Deadline: None.
Write: Clifford V. Smith, Jr., President.

German Marshall Fund of the United States, 11 Dupont Circle NW, Suite 750, Washington, DC 20036, (202) 745-3950.
Assets (yr. ended 5/91): $94,660,071 (M).
Grants: 145 grants: $4,029,148; average: $5,000-$50,000.
Purposes and activities: To contribute to the better understanding and resolution of significant common problems of industrial societies, internally and in their relations with each other.
Fields of interest: International affairs, international studies, Europe, intercultural relations, social sciences, media and communications, employment, energy, environment, foreign policy, public policy, community development, conservation, economics, immigration, political science, and history.

Types of support: Seed money, research, fellowships, special projects, publications, conferences and seminars, exchange programs, grants to individuals, continuing support, lectureships, and internships.

Limitations: Limited giving to the United States and Europe. Several exclusions. Contact funder.

Application information: Application form required only for fellowship programs.

Initial approach: Letter, telephone, or proposal.

Deadlines: November for research fellowships; March for employment fellowships; other deadlines vary.

Write: Frank E. Loy, President.

GTE Foundation, One Stamford Forum, Stamford, CT 06904, (203) 965-3620.

Assets (yr. ended 12/91): $27,054,123 (M).

Grants: 1,468 grants: $18,054,655.

Purposes and activities: Emphasis on higher education in mathematics, science and technology, and retention of minority students.

Fields of interest: Education, higher education, education—minorities, science and technology, community funds, performing arts, fine arts, museums, social services, volunteerism, and hospitals.

Types of support: Emergency funds, scholarship funds, fellowships, employee matching gifts, continuing support, employee-related scholarships, lectureships, operating budgets, special projects, and program-related investments.

Limitations: National organizations deemed to be of broad benefit to GTE companies, employees, shareholders, or customers. Giving limited to areas of company operations.

Application information: Application form required.

Initial approach: Letter or proposal.

Deadline: Summer.

Write: Maureen Gorman, Foundation VP and Secretary, and Director, Corporate Social Responsibility, GTE Corporation.

The Harris Foundation, Two North LaSalle St., Suite 605, Chicago, IL 60602-3703, (312) 621-0566.

Assets: (12/90): $18,428,937 (M).

Grants: 313 grants; average: $100-$10,000.

Purposes and activities: Interests include demonstration and research programs in prevention of family dysfunction; prevention of teenage pregnancy and infant mortality and morbidity; infant mental health and early childhood development; Jewish charities; and the arts and educational television.

Fields of interest: Child welfare, education—early childhood, child development, family services, Jewish welfare, family planning, and arts.

Types of support: Annual campaigns, seed money, special projects, research, publications, conferences and seminars, general purposes, operating budgets, scholarship funds, and equipment.

Limitations: No grants to individuals. No loans.

Application information: Application forms not required.

Initial approach: Letter.

Deadline: None.

Write: Ruth K. Belzer, Executive Director.

William Randolph Hearst Foundation, 888 Seventh Ave., 45th Fl., New York, NY 10106-0057, (212) 586-5404. Or for applications west of the Mississippi River: Thomas Eastham, VP and Western Director, 90 New Montgomery St., Suite 1212, San Francisco, CA 94105, (415) 543-0400.

Assets (yr. ended 12/31/91): $352,277,537.

Grants: $12,565,800 ($10,000-$400,000); average: $25,000-$50,000.

Purposes and activities: Programs to aid poverty-level and minority groups, and educational programs with emphasis on private secondary and higher education. Support also through two scholarship programs: Journalism Awards Program and U.S. Senate Youth Program. Favors organizations serving larger geographic areas.

Fields of interest: Education, cultural programs, health, social services, and disadvantaged.

Types of support: Scholarship funds, endowment funds, general purposes, and special projects.

Limitations: Giving only to the United States and its possessions. No grants to individuals. Other restrictions.

Application information: Only fully documented appeals will be considered. Application form not required. Application guidelines available.

Initial approach: Letter or proposal.

Deadline: None.

Board meeting date(s): March, June, September, and December.

Final notification: 4 to 6 weeks.

Write: Robert M. Frehse, Jr., VP and Executive Director (eastern applicants); or Thomas Eastham, VP and Western Director (western applicants).

The Hearst Foundation, Inc. (same addresses).

Assets (yr. ended 12/31/91): $160,755,000.

Grants: 235 grants: $6,014,000 ($10,000-$50,000).

Purposes and activities: Same as William Randolph Hearst Foundation.

Fields of interest: Same as William Randolph Hearst Foundation.

Types of support: Special projects, scholarship funds, endowment funds, general purposes, and matching funds.

Limitations: Giving limited to the United States and its possessions. No grants to individuals or private foundations.

Application information: Application guidelines. Application form not required. Only fully documented appeals will be considered.

Initial approach: Letter.

Write: Robert M. Frehse, Jr., VP and Executive Director (eastern applicants); or Thomas Eastham, VP and Western Director (western applicants).

The Hershey Foundation, P.O. Box 211, Huntsburg, OH 44046.

Assets (1/1/92): $2,069,228 (M).

Grants: 13 grants: $91,800; average: $100-$30,000.

Purposes and activities: Giving for "educational and charitable purposes with emphasis on innovative educational and cultural programs providing opportunities for children."

Fields of interest: Education, education—early childhood, elementary education, child development, and child welfare.

Types of support: Building funds, continuing support, seed money, capital campaigns, and special projects.

Limitations: Giving primarily in northeastern Ohio. No grants to individuals or for research, annual campaigns, or operating budgets.

Application information: Application form not required.

Initial approach: Letter.
Deadline: None.
Write: Debra S. Guren, President.

The Hitachi Foundation, 1509 22nd St. NW, Washington, DC 20037, (202) 457-0588.
Assets (yr. ended 4/91): $25,667,914 (M).
Grants: 92 grants: $1,489,962; average: $5,000-$30,000.

Purposes and activities: Giving in four areas: community and economic development; arts and cross-cultural understanding between Japan and the United States; education—improving the quality of teaching and learning at all levels, particularly in middle and secondary schools; and technology and human resource development—enhancing and evaluating the economic effects of rapidly changing technology, including its dysfunctional aspects, making it accessible to all segments of society, and the use of new technology in education.

Fields of interest: Community development, civic affairs, arts, Japan, education, education—minorities, elementary education, secondary education, leadership development, mathematics, science, and technology.

Types of support: General purposes, program-related investments, seed money, special projects, technical assistance, and employee matching gifts.

Limitations: No grants to individuals or religious organizations. Contact funder for other exclusions.

Application information: Application form not required.

Initial approach: Letter of no more than three pages; if project is of interest, a more detailed proposal will be invited.

Deadlines: February 1, June 1, and October 1.
Write: Dr. Del Roy.

Houston Endowment, P.O. Box 52338, Houston, TX 77052, (713) 238-8100.
Assets (1/1/92): $773,000,000.
Grants: 287 grants: $31,768,000 total; average: $1,000-$1,000,000.

Purposes and activities: For the support of any charitable, educational, or religious undertaking.

Types of support: Building funds, equipment, scholarship funds, special projects, fellowships, and continuing support.

Limitations: Giving primarily in Texas; no grants outside the continental United States. No grants to individuals; no loans.
Application information: Application form not required.
Initial approach: Letter.
Deadline: None.
Write: H. Joe Nelson III, President.

Jaquelin Hume Foundation, 550 Kearny St., Suite 1000, San Francisco, CA 94108, (415) 421-6615.
Assets (1991): $4,823,643 (M).
Grants: 28 grants: $262,863 ($250-$28,500).
Fields of interest: Education, secondary education, cultural programs, civic affairs, public policy, and economics.
Types of support: Annual campaigns, conferences and seminars, general purposes, operating budgets, and special projects.
Limitations: Giving to organizations with national impact and in California.
Application information: No required application form.
Initial approach: Letter.
Deadline: None.
Write: George H. Hume, 1st VP & Sec., or Caroline Hume, Sr. VP.

Island Foundation, 589 Mills St., Marion, MA 02738-1418, (508) 748-2809.
Assets (yr. ended 12/90): $20,228,386 (M).
Grants: 83 grants: $833,612; average: $3,000-$20,000.
Purposes and activities: Giving primarily for expanding Montessori educational practices in public schools, one of only three priorities.
Fields of interest: Community development, education, environment, youth, women, education—early childhood, social services, family planning, conservation, public policy, and human rights.
Types of support: General purposes, operating budgets, special projects, research, and program-related investments.
Limitations: Giving primarily in the northeastern United States.
Application information: See published annual report. Full proposals by invitation only.
Initial approach: Telephone or letter.
Deadlines: Rolling.
Write: Jenny D. Russell, Executive Director.

The Joyce Foundation, 135 South LaSalle St., Suite 4010, Chicago, IL 60603, (312) 782-2464.

Assets (yr. ended 12/91): $398,421,376 (M).

Grants: 355 grants: $14,398,614; average: $5,000-$50,000.

Purposes and activities: Seeks to address issues of critical regional importance, including the conservation of natural resources, the improvement of urban educational systems, the development of a prosperous and equitable economic base, the revitalization of the electoral process, and the broader acceptance of cultural diversity, with a particular concern for their impact on minorities and the poor who receive less of society's resources.

Fields of interest: Conservation, environment, ecology, cultural programs, arts, dance, performing arts, theater, economics, employment, education, elementary education, secondary education, education—minorities, vocational education, government, public policy, community development, disadvantaged, and public affairs.

Types of support: Operating budgets, continuing support, seed money, emergency funds, matching funds, consulting services, technical assistance, program-related investments, loans, special projects, publications, conferences and seminars, employee matching gifts, and general purposes.

Limitations: Giving primarily in the midwestern states, including IL, IN, IA, MI, MN, OH, and WI; limited number of conservation grants made in ND, SD, KS, MO, and NE. No grants for endowment or building funds, annual campaigns, deficit financing, research, or land acquisition.

Application information: Program policy and grant proposal guidelines reviewed annually in November. Application form required.

Initial approach: Letter.

Deadlines: November 15, March 15, July 15.

Write: Deborah Leff, President, or Joel Getzendanner, VP Programs.

W. M. Keck Foundation, 555 South Flower St., Suite 3230, Los Angeles, CA 90071, (213) 680-3833.

Assets (1992): $821,028,234 (M).

Grants: 74 grants ($45,000-$3,000,000).

Purposes and activities: To strengthen programs and studies in the earth science studies, natural resource development, medical research, and education.

Fields of interest: Engineering, medical research, biological sciences, science, and technology. Precollegiate education and arts in southern California.

Types of support: Seed money, building funds, special projects, research, scholarships, endowments, and professorships.

Limitations: Eligible accredited colleges and universities, medical schools, and major medical research institutions.

Application information: Only those organizations invited to submit a proposal will receive an applicant information form to be submitted with proposal. Application form required.

Initial approach: Letter of inquiry; unsolicited proposals not accepted.

Deadlines: March 15 and September 15 for complete proposal; initial letters accepted year-round.

Write: Sandra A. Glass for sciences, engineering, and liberal arts; and Joan DuBois for medical research, medical education, law and legal administration, arts and culture, health care, precollegiate education, and community services.

W. K. Kellogg Foundation, One Michigan Ave. East, Battle Creek, MI 49017-4058, (616) 968-1611.

Assets (yr. ended 8/91): $5,396,889,094 (M).

Grants: 1,205 grants: $144,252,139; average: $75,000-$250,000.

Purposes and activities: "To receive and administer funds for educational and charitable purposes." Aid limited to programs concerned with application of existing knowledge rather than research. Supports pilot projects that, if successful, can be continued by initiating organizations with similar problems. Projects supported are designed to improve human well-being.

Fields of interest: Youth, higher education, leadership development, health services, agriculture, rural development, community development, volunteerism, the aged, minorities, southern Africa, Latin America, Caribbean, and conservation.

Types of support: Seed money and fellowships.

Limitations: Giving primarily in the United States, Latin America, Caribbean, and southern Africa; support also for international fellowship programs in other countries. No grants to individuals (except through fellowship programs). Other exclusions. Contact funder.

Application information: Annual report and information brochure (including application guidelines). *Applications must conform to specific program priorities.* Application form not required.
Initial approach: Letter.
Deadline: None.
Write: Nancy A. Sims, Exec. Asst.—Programming.

The Joseph P. Kennedy, Jr. Foundation, 1350 New York Ave. NW, Suite 500, Washington, DC 20005-4709, (202) 393-1250.
Assets (yr. ended 12/90): $17,390,649 (M).

Grants: 24 grants: $1,442,290; average: $10,000-$50,000 to nonprofit organizations; $152,000 for grants to individuals.

Purposes and activities: The main objectives are "the prevention of mental retardation by identifying its causes and improving means by which society deals with its mentally retarded citizens." Emphasis on the use of funds in areas where a multiplier effect is possible. Awards bioethics scholarships at Georgetown University.

Fields of interest: The handicapped, biological sciences, family services, youth, the aged, AIDS, medical research, public policy, child development, health services, education—early childhood, elementary education, secondary education, employment, drug abuse, and the homeless.

Types of support: Seed money, research, special projects, conferences and seminars, consulting services, and general purposes.

Limitations: No grants for building or endowment funds, equipment, or operating budgets of schools or service organizations.

Application information: Applications considered for research projects and new models of service for persons with mental retardation and their families. Only proposals in the field of mental retardation are funded. Application form not required.
Initial approach: Two-page letter of intent.
Deadlines: Submit letter of intent prior to October 1; deadline for proposals: November 15.
Write: Eunice Kennedy Shriver, Executive Vice President.

John S. and James L. Knight Foundation, One Biscayne Tower, Suite 3800, Two S. Biscayne Blvd., Miami, FL 33131-1803, (305) 539-0009.
Assets (yr. ended 12/91): $605,039,445.

Grants: 439 grants: $25,193,263; average: $5,000-$100,000.

Purposes and activities: Four major programs: community initiatives, journalism, education, and arts and culture.

Fields of interest: Journalism, education, arts, cultural programs, community development, literacy, citizenship, the homeless, and child welfare.

Types of support: Special projects, building funds, capital campaigns, endowment funds, general purposes, matching funds, seed money, renovation projects, program-related investments, emergency funds, professorships, and fellowships.

Limitations: Giving limited to 26 communities of the Knight publishing community.

Application information: Detailed guidelines available upon request. Application form not required.

Initial approach: Letter; proposals submitted by fax not accepted.

Deadlines: January 1, April 1, July 1, and October 1.

Write: Lee Hills, Chair, or W. Gerald Austen, MD, Vice-Chair.

Koch Foundation, Inc., 2830 NW 41st St., Suite H, Gainesville, FL 32606, (904) 373-7491.

Assets (yr. ended 3/91): $98,039,109 (M).

Grants: 276 grants: $5,358,121; average: $4,000-$50,000.

Purposes and activities: Grants only for Roman Catholic religious organizations that propagate the faith.

Fields of interest: Catholic giving and religion—missionary programs.

Types of support: Operating budgets, building funds, equipment, land acquisition, and special projects.

Limitations: No support for health-related activities or social service projects. Contact funder for other exclusions.

Application information: Proposals considered at February meeting. Application form required.

Initial approach: Letter.

Deadline: December 1.

Write: Richard A. DeGraff, Executive Director.

Levi-Strauss Foundation, 1155 Battery St., San Francisco, CA 94111, (415) 544-2194.

Assets (1990): $38,781,037 (M).

Grants: 1,416 grants: $4,561,613 ($500-$75,000).

Purposes and activities: Focus on job training to enhance opportunities for disadvantaged, on job creation, on AIDS prevention, and on patient care.

Types of support: Matching funds, seed money, employee-related scholarships, technical assistance, operating budgets, and special projects.

Limitations: Giving generally limited to areas of company operation.

Initial approach: Letter.

Write: Judy Belk, Director of Contributions. Or contact regional office.

Leon Lowenstein Foundation, Inc., 126 East 56th St., 28th Fl., New York, NY 10022, (212) 319-0670, FAX: (212) 688-0134.

Assets (yr. ended 12/31/91): $74,859,596.

Grants: 100 grants: $2,398,550; average: $1,000-$25,000.

Purposes and activities: Support primarily for New York City public schools and medical research. Emphasis on child and adolescent psychiatry and Parkinson's disease.

Fields of interest: Medical research, education, secondary education, elementary education, and youth.

Types of support: General purposes, research, seed money, and special projects.

Limitations: Giving primarily in the New York City metropolitan area.

Application information: Application form not required.

Initial approach: Letter.

Deadline: None.

Final notification: 3 months.

Write: John F. Van Gorder, Executive Director.

John D. and Catherine T. MacArthur Foundation, 140 South Dearborn St., Chicago, IL 60603, (312) 726-8000.

Assets (12/90): $3,077,581,000 (M).

Grants: $115,675,981 for grants.

Purposes and activities: Seven major initiatives: MacArthur Fellows Program; the Health Program; the Community Initiatives Program; the Program on Peace and International Cooperation; the World Environment and Resources Program; the Education Program, which focuses on the promotion of literacy; and the Population Program.

Fields of interest: Health, mental health, rehabilitation, biological sciences, AIDS, media and communications, cultural programs, community development, foreign policy, public policy, international affairs, government, law and justice, arms control, conservation, ecology, environment, and education.

Types of support: Matching funds, general purposes, operating budgets, special projects, research, and fellowships.

Limitations: No support for religious programs, capital funds, conferences, or publications. Other exclusions.

Application information: Direct applications for Fellows Program not accepted. Grants increasingly initiated by the board.

Initial approach: Letter.

Deadline: None.

Write: Richard Kaplan, Director, Grants Management, Research & Information.

A. L. Mailman Family Foundation, Inc., 707 Westchester Ave., White Plains, NY 10604, (914) 681-4448, FAX: (914) 681-5182.

Assets (1/1/91): $14,962,559.

Grants: $697,875.

Purposes and activities: Support primarily for strengthening of the family with focus on disadvantaged youth; giving for educational efforts to stimulate moral and intellectual growth and development of social responsibility; and for research in and refinement of developmental individualized education.

Fields of interest: Youth, child development, education, and early childhood education.

Types of support: Seed money, matching funds, special projects, research, publications, and technical assistance.

Limitations: No grants to individuals; no operating budgets, capital or endowment funds, or continuing support for annual campaigns. No emergency funds or deficit financing.

Application information: Application form not required. Annual report, including application guidelines, available.

Initial approach: Letter.

Deadlines: Submit proposal preferably in September and February; deadline March 1 and October 1.

Board meeting dates: January and June.
Final notification: 5 months.
Write: Luba H. Lynch, Secretary.

The Marmot Foundation, 1004 Wilmington Trust Center, Wilmington, DE 19801, (302) 654-2477. Application address for Florida organizations: P.O. Box 2468, Palm Beach, FL 33480.
Assets (yr. ended 12/91): $19,615,572 (M).
Grants: 62 grants: $815,000 ($1,000-$50,000).
Purposes and activities: Support for secondary education, higher education, libraries, hospitals, youth agencies, social services, literacy programs, and environmental and ecological organizations.
Fields of interest: Family planning, higher education, secondary education, libraries, cultural programs, youth, environment, and social services.
Types of support: Research, building funds, capital campaigns, equipment, and matching funds.
Limitations: Giving primarily in Florida and Delaware. No grants to individuals or to religious organizations.
Application information: Application form not required.
Initial approach: Letter.
Deadlines: Submit proposal in April and October.
Write: Willis H. duPont, Chair (for Florida organizations); Endsley P. Fairman, Secretary (for Delaware organizations).

Mattel Foundation, c/o Mattel Toys, 333 Continental Blvd., El Segundo, CA 90245, (213) 524-3530.
Assets (1990): $1,000,000 (M).
Grants: $823,000.
Purposes and activities: Grants for care and special education of children in areas of company operation; support also for international programs, including relief projects throughout Asia, Europe, and South America, and for employee matching gifts to higher education.
Fields of interest: Education, educational associations, elementary education, child welfare, Asia, Australia, Belgium, Canada, Europe, France, Italy, Japan, Latin America, Mexico, Scotland, Southeast Asia, South Pacific, Spain, Poland, Portugal, United Kingdom, and Venezuela.

Types of support: Operating budgets, seed money, special projects, emergency funds, general purposes, in-kind gifts, and employee-related scholarships.

Limitations: Giving nationally and internationally to groups only. No individuals. No research funds. No grants to programs receiving substantial financial support from federal, state, or local government agencies.

Application information: Application form not required.

Initial approach: Letter or telephone.

Write: Janice R. Nakayama, Administrator.

McKesson Foundation, Inc., One Post St., San Francisco, CA 94104, (415) 983-8673.

Assets (1992): $9,688,026 (M).

Grants: 294 grants: $1,843,896; average: $5,000-$25,000.

Purposes and activities: Giving primarily to programs for junior high school students, and for emergency services such as food and shelter; limited support for other educational, civic, cultural, and human service programs.

Fields of interest: Secondary education, education—minorities, health, cultural programs, education, elementary education, welfare, civic affairs, youth, disadvantaged, child welfare, child development, and delinquency.

Types of support: Continuing support, emergency funds, employee matching gifts, matching funds, operating budgets, seed money, employee-related scholarships, and equipment.

Limitations: Giving primarily in San Francisco, California, or where company has a major presence.

Application information: Application form not required.

Initial approach: Letter.

Deadline: Submit between April and October; submit full proposal upon request.

Write: Marcia M. Argyris, President.

Eugene and Agnes E. Meyer Foundation, 1400 16th St. NW, Suite 360, Washington, DC 20036, (202) 483-8294.

Assets (yr. ended 12/90): $55,984,614 (M).

Grants: $2,100,347; average: $10,000-$25,000.

Purposes and activities: Grants principally for education, neighborhood development/housing, health and mental health, the arts and humanities, law and justice, and community service. The foundation also administers the Metropolitan Washington Community AIDS Partnership.

Fields of interest: Education, health, mental health, AIDS, law and justice, housing, community development, arts, humanities, and social services.

Types of support: Seed money, matching funds, special projects, technical assistance, continuing support, operating budgets, and general purposes.

Limitations: Giving limited to Washington, DC area, including Virginia and Maryland. No grants to individuals or for national or international programs. Contact funder for other exclusions.

Application information: Read annual report grants list and grant guidelines. Application form not required.

Initial approach: Two-page letter of inquiry.

Deadlines: April 1, August 1, and December 1.

Write: Julie L. Rogers, President.

Motorola Foundation, Inc., 1303 East Algonquin Rd., Schaumburg, IL 60196, (708) 576-6200.

Assets (yr. ended 12/90): $1,116,860 (M).

Grants: 439 grants: $2,838,885; average: $1,000-$5,000.

Purposes and activities: Giving for higher and other education, including an employee matching gift program, united funds, and hospitals; support also for cultural programs, social services, and youth agencies.

Fields of interest: Education, higher education, science and technology, community funds, hospitals, cultural programs, youth, and social services.

Types of support: Operating budgets, building funds, scholarship funds, employee matching gifts, fellowships, general purposes, and continuing support.

Limitations: Giving primarily in communities where the company has major facilities, with emphasis on Chicago, IL; Huntsville, AL; Mt. Pleasant, IA; Phoenix, AZ; Austin, Fort Worth, and Sequin, TX; and Fort Lauderdale and Boynton Beach, FL. No support for religious organizations or secondary schools (except for the employee matching gift program). No grants to individuals. Other exclusions.

Application information: Application form not required.
Initial approach: Letter, proposal, or telephone.
Write: Pamela Cox, Administrator.

NEC Foundation of America, c/o NEC America Inc., Eight Old Sod Farm Rd., Melville, NY 11747, (516) 753-7021, FAX: (516) 753-7096.

Assets (4/1/92): $9,473,635 (M).

Grants: 6 grants: $190,000 ($5,000-$40,000).

Purposes and activities: Focus on the integration of computers and communications (C&C) "to encourage synergy between (a) science and technology education, principally at the secondary level; and (b) efforts to apply technology to assist people with disabilities."

Fields of interest: Science and technology, handicapped, engineering, computer sciences, secondary education, and mathematics.

Types of support: Publications, seed money, general purposes, special projects, conferences and seminars, and research.

Limitations: Giving only for programs or groups with immediate national reach and impact. No support for individual elementary, secondary schools, or school districts. Contact funder for list.

Application information: Informational brochure. Application form not required.

Initial approach: One-page preliminary proposal in advance of full proposal.

Deadlines: November 1 and May 1.

Board meeting: Quarterly.

Final notification: 4 to 6 weeks after receipt of proposal.

Write: Sylvia Clark, Executive Director.

The OMC Foundation, 100 Sea Horse Dr., Waukegan, IL 60085, (708) 689-5483.

Assets (yr. ended 6/90): $3,942,387 (M).

Grants: 43 grants: $42,000; average: $500-$1,000.

Purposes and activities: Support of private higher education, especially business and engineering, in states in which the company operates, scholarship aid to children of company employees, and capital grants to hospital and cultural building projects in company locations; support also for recreation and environmental programs.

Fields of interest: Higher education, business education, engineering, secondary education, hospitals, cultural programs, environment, and recreation.

Types of support: Continuing support, annual campaigns, seed money, building funds, equipment, special projects, research, scholarship funds, capital campaigns, and renovation projects.

Limitations: Limited to areas of company operations: AR, FL, GA, IL, IN, MI, MO, NC, NY, OR, SC, TN, TX, and WI. Other exclusions.

Application information: Application form not required.

Initial approach: Letter.

Deadline: Submit proposal preferably in August; September 30 deadline.

Write: Mr. Laurin M. Baker, Director, Public Affairs.

Pacific Telesis Foundation, Pacific Telesis Ctr., 130 Kearny St., Rm. 3309, San Francisco, CA 94108, (415) 394-3769.

Assets (1991): $62,421,542 (M).

Grants: 316 grants: $7,500,658.

Purposes and activities: Support primarily for elementary and secondary education reform, higher education, culture, community funds, and community and civic affairs.

Fields of interest: Education, education—early childhood, elementary education, secondary education, higher education, minority education, the aged, youth, women, the handicapped, drug abuse, and AIDS.

Types of support: Publications, special projects, seed money, employee matching gifts, matching funds, and technical assistance.

Limitations: Giving primarily in states where company does business. No support for organizations receiving United Way support. No grants to individual schools. Call to check qualifying factors.

Application information: Application form not required.

Initial approach: Letter.

Deadline: None.

Write: Jere A. Jacobs, President.

The David and Lucile Packard Foundation, 300 Second St., Suite 200, Los Altos, CA 94022, (415) 948-7658.

Assets (12/91): $718,175,870 (M).

Grants: 365 grants: $29,297,988; average: $5,000-$50,000.

Purposes and activities: Elementary and secondary education, child development, early childhood education, minority education, employment and job training, the disadvantaged, the homeless, housing, community development, conservation, environment, ecology, family planning, and Latin America.

Types of support: National giving for education. Seed money, internships, research, fellowships, special projects, consulting services, renovation projects, technical assistance, operating expenses, loans, equipment, building funds, and land acquisition.

Limitations: Giving to the arts only in California.

Application information: Application form not required.

Initial approach: Submit one copy of proposal.

Deadlines: December 15, March 15, June 15, September 15.

Write: Colburn S. Wilbur, Executive Director.

J. C. Penney Corporate Giving Program, P.O. Box 659000, Dallas, TX 75265-9000, (214) 519-1320.

Grants awarded (2/1/91): $20,600,000 total.

Purposes and activities: Funding emphasis is given to projects; organizations that serve a broad sector of the community; national projects that benefit local organizations across the country; organizations that provide direct services to their clients; and projects and organizations with a proven record of success.

Fields of interest: Elementary education, early childhood education, secondary education, volunteerism, youth, vocational education, minority education, higher education, health, social services, drug abuse, cultural programs, civic affairs, and arts.

Types of support: Donated equipment, donated products, use of facilities, and employee volunteer services.

Limitations: Giving limited to the 50 states of the United States.

Application information: Application form not required. Corporate report, corporate giving report, and application guidelines available.

Initial approach: Letter.

Deadline: None.

Write: David Lenz, VP, J. C. Penney Fund, and Manager, Corp. Public Affairs, and Robin Caldwell, Corp. Contributions Manager.

The Procter & Gamble Company Corporate Giving Program, P.O. Box 599, Cincinnati, OH 45201.

Total giving: $16,680,000.

Grants: $7,300,000; includes $5,433,000 for in-kind gifts.

Purposes and activities: Support for education, including research and development and engineering fellowships and grants to colleges and universities; social service agencies and civic groups; support for equal opportunity and minority recruitment programs; and support for secondary education programs.

Fields of interest: Business education, drug abuse, education, handicapped, health, minorities, secondary education, community development, health associations, and hunger social services.

Types of support: Fellowships, in-kind gifts, research, donated products, loaned talent, annual campaigns, donated land, and capital campaigns.

Limitations: Giving limited to headquarters and areas of company operations.

Write: R. R. Fitzpatrick, Manager, Contributions.

The Procter & Gamble Fund, P.O. Box 599, Cincinnati, OH 45201, (513) 983-3913.

Assets (6/30/91): $47,611,925 (M).

Grants: 5,371 grants ($50-$1,880,000); average: $5,000-$100,000.

Purposes and activities: Grants nationally for private higher education, youth, community funds, handicapped, urban affairs, civic affairs, hospitals, public policy research organizations, educational associations, youth, and civic affairs.

Types of support: Annual campaigns, building funds, continuing support, emergency funds, equipment, land acquisition, matching funds, employee-related scholarships, and matching gifts.

Limitations: Giving in areas in the United States and where the company and subsidiaries have large concentrations of employees; national giving for higher education and economic public affairs. No grants to individuals.

Application information: Application form not required.

Write: R. R. Fitzpatrick, Vice President and Secretary.

Reebok Foundation, 100 Technology Center Dr., Stoughton, MA 02702.

Assets (yr. ended 12/90): $3,877,615 (M).

Grants: 81 grants: $1,062,849; average: $5,000-$50,000.

Purposes and activities: The foundation's purpose is to promote individual freedom of expression and social change and to challenge others to help solve society's common problems. This can be best done at the present time through two channels: the distribution of cash grants to organizations with deserving programs or projects in such areas as education, human rights, cultural affairs, and social services; and the promotion of volunteerism and other community participation by its employees. The foundation established the Reebok Human Rights Award, which recognizes people under 30 who have advanced the course of human rights.

Fields of interest: Human rights, civil rights, freedom, peace, public policy, intercultural relations, international studies, southern Africa, urban development, education, higher education, secondary education, social services, women, minorities, family services, arts, humanities, Catholic giving, and Jewish giving.

Types of support: Capital campaigns, in-kind gifts, annual campaigns, conferences and seminars, operating budgets, loaned talent, professorships, renovation projects, donated products, internships, endowment funds, general purposes, matching funds, public relations services, and scholarship funds.

Limitations: Giving primarily in areas of company operations. No giving to individuals.

Application information: Application guidelines. Application form required.

Initial approach: Letter.

Write: Jean Mahoney-Culbreath, Exec. Dir.

Rockefeller Brothers Fund, 1290 Avenue of the Americas, New York, NY 10104, (212) 373-4200.

Assets (12/31/91): $317,926,715 (M).

Grants: 209 grants: $10,887,465 ($1,000-$250,000); average: $25,000-$300,000.

Purposes and activities: Supports efforts of United States and abroad that encourage global interdependence. Five major giving categories: (a) one world—focusing on world security and world resources, (b) New York City, (c) nonprofit sector, (d) education, and (e) special concerns: South Africa.

Fields of interest: International development, education, education—minorities, arms control, conservation, environment, intercltural relations, agriculture, economics, urban development, AIDS, and southern Africa.

Types of support: General purposes, seed money, special projects, conferences and seminars, internships, exchange programs, matching funds, consulting services, continuing support, technical assistance, and research.

Limitations: No support for churches, hospitals, or community centers. No grants to individuals (including research) with two exceptions: (a) the RBF Fellowships and (b) the Program for Asian Projects. No grants for land or building funds and no loans.

Application information: Application form not required.

Initial approach: Letter no more than two or three pages.

Deadline: None.

Board meetings: February, June, and November.

Final notification: 3 months.

Write: Benjamin R. Shute, Jr., Secretary-Treasurer.

The Rockefeller Foundation, 1133 Avenue of the Americas, New York, NY 10036, (212) 869-8500.

Assets (12/31/91): $2,171,548,237 (M).

Grants: 915 grants: $68,409,950 ($357-$1,750,000).

Purposes and activities: Grants and fellowships offered in three areas: international science-based development, arts and humanities, and equal opportunities. Also smaller grants in U.S. school reform and international security. Holds conferences of international scope and residencies for artists and scholars.

Types of support: Fellowships, research, publications, conferences and seminars, special projects, grants to individuals, seed money, technical assistance, and so on.

Limitations: No support to establish local hospitals, churches, schools, libraries, or welfare agencies or building or operating funds; financing altruistic movements involving private profit; or attempts to influence legislation. No grants for personal aid to individuals or for capital or endowment funds, general support, or scholarships; no loans.

Application information: Application forms required for certain programs and fellowships. Information on affirmative action efforts of organization may be requested, including data on gender and minority composition of the institution's leadership. Annual report, program policy statement, and application guidelines available.

Initial approach: Letter.

Deadline: None unless specified in special notices for certain programs and fellowships. Board meets usually in March, June, September, and December.

Write: Lynda Mullen, Secretary.

The Winthrop Rockefeller Foundation, 308 East Eighth St., Little Rock, AR 72202, (501) 376-6854.

Assets: $55,348,857 (M).

Grants (1990): 127 grants ($325-$348,000); average: $1,000-$50,000.

Fields of interest: Education, higher education, educational research, literacy, citizenship, public policy, civic affairs, and agriculture.

Types of support: Special projects, seed money, conferences and seminars, matching funds, technical assistance, consulting services, publications, and program-related investments.

Limitations: Giving primarily in Arkansas or to projects that benefit Arkansas.

Application information: Application form required.

Initial approach: Telephone or letter.

Deadlines: Submit proposal by January 1 or July 1.

Write: Mahlon Martin, President.

The Ryder System Charitable Foundation, Inc., c/o Ryder System, Inc., 3600 NW 82nd Ave., Miami, FL 33166, (305) 593-3642.

Assets (yr. ended 12/90): $1,093,446 (M).

Grants: 306 grants: $2,336,453; average: $1,000-$30,000.

Purposes and activities: Grants for health and human services; educational, cultural, civic, and literary organizations that operate in communities having significant concentrations of Ryder personnel; giving also for the advancement of minorities and disadvantaged groups.

Fields of interest: Health services, arts, cultural programs, civic affairs, community development, social services, minorities, disadvantaged, higher education, elementary education, minorities education, and secondary education.

Types of support: Employee matching gifts, annual campaigns, operating budgets, scholarship funds, and in-kind gifts.

Limitations: Given primarily in areas of company operations: southern Florida; Atlanta, Georgia; Detroit, Michigan; St. Louis, Missouri; Cincinnati, Ohio; and Dallas, Texas.

Application information: Application form not required.

Initial approach: Letter.

Deadline: lst half of calendar year.

Write: Office of Corporate Programs.

The San Francisco Foundation, 685 Market St., Suite 910, San Francisco, CA 94105-9716, (415) 495-3100.

Assets (6/91): $226,099,459.

Grants: 55 grants to individuals: $277,000; average: $1,000-$10,000.

Purposes and activities: Grants in education, arts and humanities, community health, environment, and urban affairs.

Fields of interest: Education, AIDS, child welfare, youth, the homeless, environment, community affairs, and performing arts.

Types of support: Seed money, operating budgets, loans, technical assistance, and special projects.

Limitations: Giving limited to the Bay Area of California.

Application information: Application form required.

Initial approach: Letter of intent (not exceeding three pages).

Deadline: Letters reviewed continuously.

Write: Robert M. Fisher, Director.

Scott Paper Company Foundation, One Scott Plaza, Philadelphia, PA 19113, (610) 522-6160.

Assets (12/31/91): $5,389 (M).

Grants: 87 to individuals; average: $1,000-$3,500.

Purposes and activities: Primary focus on helping children in Scott communities "reach their full potential" through grants in education.

Fields of interest: Youth, child development, early childhood education, secondary education, literacy, disadvantaged, and Europe.

Types of support: Seed money, employee-related scholarships, consulting services, continuing support, emergency funds, equipment, matching funds, special projects, and technical assistance.

Limitations: Giving limited to areas of major company operations in PA, DE, WA, NY, MS, WI, AL, MI, AR, and ME. Other limitations.

Application information: Application form required.
Initial approach: Letter requesting guidelines.
Board meetings: June and December.
Final notification: 3 months.
Write: Fran Rizzardi Urso, Manager, Corporate Contributions.

The Sears-Roebuck Foundation, Sears Tower, Dept. 903-BSC 51-02, Chicago, IL 60684, (312) 875-8337.
Assets (1/91): $3,463,546 (M).
Grants: 16 grants: $2,716,853 ($1,000-$1,423,928).
Purposes and activities: The foundation funds specific national programs related to workforce readiness and volunteerism among employees; community programs are supported by local Sears units. To be considered national, a program or organization must serve constituents in multiple states, not limited to a specific geographic location.
Fields of interest: Education, higher education, education—early childhood, elementary education, secondary education, education—minorities, literacy, vocational education, and volunteerism.
Types of support: Special projects and seed money.
Limitations: No support for religious groups. Other exclusions.
Application information: Application form not required.
Initial approach: Request guidelines.
Deadline: None.
Write: Paula A. Banks, President and Executive Director.

Smart Family Foundation, 15 Benders Dr., Greenwich, CT 06831, (203) 531-1474.
Assets (yr. ended 12/90): $49,216,276.
Grants: 25 grants: $2,319,179; average: $10,000-$120,000.
Purposes and activities: The foundation is primarily interested in education projects and, in particular, has been focusing on projects that affect primary and secondary school children.
Fields of interest: Education, secondary education, and elementary education.
Types of support: Research, seed money, and program-related investment.
Limitations: No grants to individuals.
Application information: Application form not required.

Initial approach: Proposal or letter.
Deadline: 90 days prior to meetings.
Write: Raymond Smart, President.

The Richard W. Sorenson Family Foundation, 6540 SE Harbor Circle, Stuart, FL 34996. Application address: 60 Johnson Ave., Plainville, CT 06062.
Assets (yr. ended 12/90): $2,266,639 (M).
Grants: 14 grants ($100-$10,000).
Purposes and activities: Support primarily for private schools; some grants for general charitable purposes.
Fields of interest: Secondary education and general charitable giving.
Application information: Application form required.
Initial approach: Letter requesting application materials.
Deadline: July 1.
Write: Richard W. Sorenson, President and Treasurer.

Sprint Foundation, 2330 Shawnee Mission Pkwy., Westwood, KS 66205, (913) 624-3343. Mailing address: P.O. Box 11315, Kansas City, MO 64112.
Assets (12/91): $9,604,379 (M).
Grants: 79 grants: $1,125,225 ($225-$235,000).
Purposes and activities: Emphasis on education, including business education, secondary education, and higher education; performing arts and youth; and support also for community development and drug abuse programs.
Fields of interest: Education, business education, education—minorities, secondary education, higher education, performing arts, youth community development, and drug abuse.
Types of support: Annual campaigns, employee matching gifts, capital campaigns, special projects, fellowships, and general purposes.
Limitations: Giving primarily in headquarters city and subsidiary locations: CA, GA, KS, MO, TX, VA, and Washington, DC.
Application information: Application form not required.
Initial approach: Brief letter or proposal.
Deadline: None.
Write: Don G. Forsythe, VP, Corporate Relations.

Janet Upjohn Stearns Charitable Trust, c/o Morgan Guaranty Trust Co., P.O. Box 8714, Wilmington, DE 19899-8714, (212) 826-7700. Application address: c/o Morgan Guaranty Trust Co. of New York, Nine West 57th St., New York, NY 10019.

Assets (yr. ended 12/90): $1,509,465 (M).

Grants: 35 grants: $62,000 ($500-$15,000).

Fields of interest: Secondary education, higher education, museums, social services, cultural programs, and health associations.

Application information: Application form not required.

Deadline: None.

Advisory committee: Robin Munn Aldie, Janet T. Beck, G. E. Eisenhardt, Janet W. Ley.

Trustee: Morgan Guaranty Trust Co. of New York.

Stuart Foundation, The Embarcadero, Suite 420, San Francisco, CA 94105, (415) 495-1144.

Assets (12/90): $163,734,985 (M).

Grants: 148 grants: $7,216,571; average: $10,000-$50,000.

Purposes and activities: Prevention of child abuse and neglect, strengthening the foster care system, strengthening public schools, preventing school failure, and preventing teenage pregnancy.

Fields of interest: Education—early childhood, elementary education, education, child welfare, family services, and youth.

Types of support: Seed money, operating budgets.

Limitations: Giving primarily in California and Washington. No individual grants.

Application information: Application form not required.

Initial approach: Letter or telephone.

Deadlines: 3 months prior to board meeting dates: March, June, September, and December.

Write: Theodore E. Lobman, President.

T. L. Temple Foundation, 109 Temple Blvd., Lufkin, TX 75901, (409) 639-5197.

Assets (12/30/91): $260,000,000.

Grants: 98 grants: $11,000,000; average: $1,000-$55,000.

Purposes and activities: Support for education, health, and social and community services.

Fields of interest: Education, higher education, adult education, early childhood education, elementary education, health services, cultural programs, drug abuse, disadvantaged, and hospices. Others.

Types of support: Emergency funds, building funds, equipment, matching funds, scholarships, special projects, research, and general.

Limitations: Giving primarily in East Texas counties. No support for religious organizations. No loans or deficit financing.

Application information: Application form required. Guidelines, program policy statement, 990-PF.

Initial approach: Letter.

Deadline: None.

Write: M. F. Buddy Zeagler, Deputy Executive Director.

The Trull Foundation, 404 Fourth St., Palacios, TX 77465, (512) 972-5241.

Assets (1/1/91): $14,976,665 (M).

Grants: 209 grants: $690,560 total ($60-$15,000); average: $5,000.

Purposes and activities: Primarily support to children's welfare organizations and minorities; elementary, secondary, and higher education. Emphasis on religious schools, literacy programs, child development, and youth agencies. Some support for Hispanic concerns.

Fields of interest: Elementary education, secondary education, higher education, youth population studies, AIDS, and the aged.

Types of support: Operating budgets, continuing support, annual campaigns, seed money, equipment, professorships, internships, scholarships, special projects, publications, conferences and seminars, fellowships, consulting services, general purposes, renovation projects, and technical assistance.

Limitations: Giving primarily in southern Texas. No grants to individuals and rarely for building or endowment funds; no loans.

Application information: Biennial report, including application guidelines. Application not required.

Initial approach: Letter.

Deadline: None.

Write: Colleen Claybourn, Executive Director.

The UPS Foundation, 400 Perimeter Ctr., Terraces North, Atlanta, GA 30346, (404) 913-6451.

Assets (yr. ended 12/91): $48,000,000 (M).

Grants: 248 grants: $7,962,809; average: $5,000-$50,000.

Purposes and activities: Emphasis on adult literacy; food to hungry Americans; economic opportunity for minorities; programs for the handicapped; and support for higher education, including academic, public policy, and transportation and logistics research.

Fields of interest: Welfare, youth, child welfare, disadvantaged, welfare—indigent individuals, hunger, the aged, higher education, adult education, education—minorities, AIDS, public policy, civic affairs, transportation, and Canada.

Types of support: Continuing support, seed money, equipment, matching funds, professorships, internships, scholarship funds, employee-related scholarships, fellowships, special projects, and research.

Limitations: No religious support. No grants to individuals.

Application information: Application form not required.

Initial approach: Letter, preferably no more than two pages addressing programs, objectives, and cost.

Deadlines: Submit proposal January through August.

Write: Clement E. Hanrahan, Executive Director.

US West Foundation, 7800 East Orchard Rd., Suite 300, Englewood, CO 80111, (303) 793-6661. Application address: Local US West Public Relations Office.

Assets (1/91): $13,853,911.

Grants: 2,596 grants: $13,853,913; average: $500-$10,000.

Purposes and activities: Giving for health and human services, including programs for minorities and youth; early childhood, elementary, secondary, higher education, rural and community development; and cultural programs.

Fields of interest: Disadvantaged, leadership development, minorities, the homeless, Native Americans, volunteerism, youth, AIDS, education, higher education, business education, secondary education, education—early childhood, education—minorities, elementary education, community development, rural development, and cultural programs.

Types of support: Operating budgets, general purposes, employee matching gifts, special projects, continuing support, matching funds, seed money, and technical assistance.

Limitations: Giving restricted to states served by US West calling areas: AZ, CO, IA, ID, MN, MT, ND, NE, NM, SD, OR, UT, WA, and WY. No grants to individuals or for scholarships, endowment funds, or athletic funds. Contact funder for all exclusions.
Application information: Application form not required.
Initial approach: Proposal.
Deadline: None.
Write: Larry J. Nash, Director of Administration.

Weingart Foundation, 1055 West Seventh St., Suite 3050, Los Angeles CA 90117-1984, (213) 688-7799. Mailing Address: P.O. Box 17982, Los Angeles, CA 90117-0982.

Assets (6/91): $458,795,070 (M).

Grants: 323 grants: $22,686,999; average: $10,000-$250,000.

Purposes and activities: Support for community services; health and medicine; higher education, including a student loan program; and public policy, with emphasis on programs for children and youth.

Fields of interest: Social services, higher education, secondary education, elementary education, early childhood education, minorities, youth, child development, child welfare, and hospitals.

Types of support: Seed money, building funds, special projects, matching funds, renovation projects, student loans, capital campaigns, and equipment.

Limitations: Southern California only. No individuals.

Application information: Student loan program limited to 14 private colleges and universities in southern California. Application form required.

Initial approach: Letter.
Deadline: None.
Write: Charles W. Jacobson, President.

Glossary

Annual appeals: Nonprofit efforts to obtain yearly gifts

Annual Report: A report issued by a foundation or corporation that provides financial data and describes grantmaking activities

Assets: Resources of the foundation or giver

Beneficiary: The recipient of a grant

Building funds: Organized capital campaigns

Capital campaign: A long-range building or endowment campaign

Community foundation: A regional organization established as nonprofit that derives funds from many sources that are then held in an endowment that is independently administered to make grants

Conferences and seminars: Covers conference or seminar expenses

Consulting services: Foundation staff provides consulting services to grantee or evaluates grantee services; not a cash award

Continuing Support: A regularly renewed grant

Contract: A legal agreement that specifies the services to be provided and expected outcomes to be achieved within an agreed time frame in exchange for resources awarded

Cooperative venture: A joint grantmaking partnership between funders who share in various responsibilities

Debt reduction: A grant to reduce indebtedness of grantee

Donor: The funding source that has the potential to fund your idea within the realm of possibilities

172 GRANTWRITING, FUNDRAISING, AND PARTNERSHIPS

Donor research: The process of seeking the donor and doing the necessary homework to make the contact successful

Emergency grant: An one-time grant to cover an emergency

Employee matching: A contribution by employer to match employee's gift

Employee-related scholarships: A scholarship program for employees' children funded by a company-sponsored foundation

Endowment: Funds that are permanently invested for income purposes

Endowment fund: A permanent gift intended for investment for income purposes

Equipment: An equipment purchase grant

Exchange grants: Grants that support international programs

Family foundation: A private, independent foundation funded by a single family

Federated giving program: A giving program administered by an "umbrella" organization that then awards funds to several nonprofit agencies (e.g., United Way)

Fellowships: Directly awarded institutional funds for research

501 (c)(3): The IRS definition of tax-exempt, nonprofit, public charities, private operating foundations, and private nonoperating foundations

Form 990-PF: The annual information return form required of all private foundations by the IRS; requires information on assets, income, operating expenses, contributions and grants, paid staff and salaries, program funding areas, grantmaking guidelines and restrictions, and procedures for grant applications

General-purpose grants: Unrestricted grants made to assist an organization's work

Grant: A sum of money awarded to a person or agency to address a problem or need

Grantee financial report: A detailed financial report that specifies the expenditures of grant funds

Grants for professorship: A grant to a university for endowment of a chair

In-kind contributions: Grants or gifts of property, time, personnel, or equipment usually donated by the grantee in place of grants or money

Internships: Funds awarded specifically to an institution, not an individual, for internship purposes

Lectureship: Grants to educational institutions for lectures

Loans: Monetary awards that must be repaid

Matching funds: Cash or in-kind contributions of the grantee to match part of the recipient's gift; if the grantee allows indirect costs, be sure to compute this on all local contributions because this is part of the match

Matching grant: A grant that matches funds from another donor(s)

Operating budgets: Grants to cover day-to-day overhead expenses

Operating foundation: A private, nonprofit foundation that uses its funds to conduct its own social or research programs

Payout requirement: The minimum amount required of private foundations for charitable expenditures, including grants and administrative costs of grantmaking. A foundation is annually required to pay out 5% or more of the average market value of the foundation's assets

Private foundation: A nonprofit organization that has its own funds and programs managed by trustees or directors and established for charitable activities, primarily accomplished through the award of grants; meets IRS code definition for section 501 (c)(3)

Program funds: Funds administered internally by the foundation or corporate giving program to support a program

Program officer: A foundation staff member who reviews and processes grant applications for the board of trustees

Proposal: The written document developed to apply for funding

Public charity: A tax-exempt organization under IRS Code 501 (c)(3) classified by IRS as a public charity and not a private foundation

Publication grant: A grant to fund publications of interest to the foundation

Qualifying expenditures: Private foundation expenditures that satisfy payout requirement; includes grants, administrative expenses, set-asides, loans and program-related investments, and amounts used to carry out exempt purposes

Query letter: A brief letter outlining an individual's or organization's activities and its needs for funding; the letter is sent to determine whether a full proposal should be submitted to a grantmaker

Renovation grants: Awards for remodeling or rehabilitation of property

Research grant: Funds awarded to institutions that cover investigation costs

Scholarship funds: Grants to an institution for support of undergraduate students

Seed money: Money used to begin a new project; it may cover salaries and other operating expenses for a planning and development effort

Set-asides: Funds that are designated for special purposes by a foundation to qualify toward its annual payout requirement, to be paid within a 5-year period

Special project grants: Grants that support specific projects

Student aid: Direct awards to individuals—scholarships or grants

Student loans: Educational loans made directly to students

Technical assistance: Services of a specialist offered to an institution by a funder

Trustee: A member of the foundation's governing board who reviews grant proposals and makes decisions; also called a "board member" or "director"

Bibliography

Books

Brewer, E. W., Achilles, C. M., & Fuhriman, J. R. (1993). *Finding funding: Grantwriting for the financially challenged educator.* Newbury Park, CA: Corwin.

Brewer, E. W., Achilles, C. M., & Fuhriman, J. (1995). *Finding funding: Grantwriting and project management from start to finish* (2nd ed.). Thousand Oaks, CA: Corwin.

Coley, S. M., & Scheinberg, C. A. (1990). *Proposal writing.* Newbury Park, CA: Sage.

Foundation Center. (1993a). *Foundation directory, 1993 edition.* New York: Author.

Foundation Center. (1993b). *Foundation directory supplement.* New York: Author.

Foundation Center. (1993c). *Grants for elementary and secondary education.* New York: Author.

Foundation Center. (1993d). *The national guide to funding for elementary and secondary education.* New York: Author.

Foundation Center. (1993e). *The national guide to funding for the economically disadvantaged.* New York: Author.

Foundation Center. (1994a). *The annual register of grant support.* New York: Author.

Foundation Center. (1994b). *The foundation 1000.* New York: Author.

Foundation Center. (1995). *Foundation directory, 1995 edition.* New York: Author.

Lauffer, A. (1983). *Grantsmanship* (2nd ed.). Beverly Hills, CA: Sage.

Lauffer, A. (1984). *Grantsmanship and fundraising.* Beverly Hills, CA: Sage.

Parnell, D. (1985). *The neglected majority.* Washington, DC: The Community College Press.

Ruskin, K. (1988). *Voluntary support of colleges of education at doctoral institutions.* Unpublished doctoral dissertation, Northern Illinois University, DeKalb.
The Taft Group. (1982). *The Taft corporate directory.* Rockville, MD: Author.
The Taft Group. (1990). *Corporate giving directory.* Rockville, MD: Author.
The Taft Group. (1994). *Foundation reporter 1995.* Rockville, MD: Author.

Other Publications

Directory of Financial Aids for Minorities
TGC/Reference Service Press
1100 Industrial Road, Suite #9
San Carlos, CA 94070

Education Grants Alert
Capitol Publications
P.O. Box 1453
Alexandria, VA 22313-2053

The Chronicle of Philanthropy
P.O. Box 1955
Marion, OH 43306-2055

The Grantsmanship Center News
P.O. Box 17220
Los Angeles, CA 90017

The U.S. Department of Education: Advance Grant Calendar; 24-hour Electronic Bulletin Board: Offers information about application deadlines, range, and number of awards and program contact. Grants and Contracts Service, USDOE, Room 3616, 7th & D Sts., Washington, DC. Attn: George Wagner, (202) 708-8773.

Index

CORWIN
PRESS

The Corwin Press logo—a raven striding across an open book—represents the happy union of courage and learning. We are a professional-level publisher of books and journals for K–12 educators, and we are committed to creating and providing resources that embody these qualities. Corwin's motto is "Success for All Learners."